THE LAMB WILL NOT BE SILENCED

BETTY LIBER

CREATION HOUSE
A STRANG COMPANY

THE LAMB WILL NOT BE SILENCED by Betty Liber
Published by Creation House
A Strang Company
600 Rinehart Road
Lake Mary, Florida 32746
www.creationhouse.com

Unless otherwise noted, all Scripture quotations are from the Holy Bible, New International Version. Copyright ©1973, 1978, 1984, International Bible Society. Used by permission.

Scripture quotations marked KJV are from the King James Version of the Bible.

Scripture quotations marked RSV are from the Revised Standard Version of the Bible. Copyright © 1946, 1952, 1971 by the Division of Christian Education of the National Council of the Churches of Christ in the USA. Used by permission.

Scripture quotations marked NEW JERUSALEM BIBLE are from *The New Jerusalem Bible*. Copyright 1999 by Doubleday, a division of Random House, New York.

Cover design by Terry Clifton

Library of Congress Control Number: 2005930408
International Standard Book Number: 1-59185-888-7

First Edition

05 06 07 08 09— 987654321
Printed in the United States of America

This book is dedicated to my beloved grandfather, Joseph Herman, who raised my sister and me with firm but loving discipline, and whose quiet yet uncompromising faith in God led me to our Savior Jesus Christ.

CONTENTS

ACKNOWLEDGMENTS

I WISH TO ACKNOWLEDGE and thank my daughter, Cindy Hower, whose computer expertise helped me to complete this manuscript. Love ya!

INTRODUCTION

T HE IMPETUS FOR writing this book came from one of the most dynamic life-changing experiences of my existence. The title for the first chapter is from the poem "Transfiguration," which God gave me the power to express in 1965, shortly after my encounter with Christ.

The transfiguration referred to in my poem was not the first supernatural happening in my life, nor was it the last, but it is the reason my voice will not be silenced in giving glory and honor to both the Father and the Son, for a long as I live.

Up to this point, I have been very close-mouthed about my spiritual encounters because, frankly, there were not many people with whom I thought I could entrust this information. Even my own family has not known most of the details—after all, I'm just "Mom" to them. Also, I knew that in my life's journey to serve God, I would encounter many jealous scorners and unbelievers who would brush aside the messages God sent through me to awaken and guide others to see a more beautiful side of faith.

God now has released me, however, from my silence and is urging me to boldly share this information. The time has come to give both warnings (people sure don't like that) and the HOPE for the end times in which we live. It is now clear that God has called and anointed me to be a prophet that shakes up the conventional organized church that has fallen asleep to the lull of their sorely incomplete definition of holiness and goodness. Sadly, the dangerous deficiency of this religiosity is all that many people comprehend, resulting in a lack of awareness of the spiritual level to which God is calling His children.

Since I am average in many ways, I often have wondered why God has chosen to call me to be His messenger. Maybe it is because I have always stood my ground against anything and anyone who would attempt to minimize the significance of God, His beloved Son, or His Holy Word. Or maybe, as Jesus said, it is because God chooses the simple, or less educated, to confound the wise! Or maybe, my testimony of what I have seen and heard will ignite a passion for God in people who have not yet had these same kinds of experiences firsthand.

Because I have looked into His magnificent eyes, I can knowingly say to you, my friend: There is eternal love in the windows of His soul. In those eyes, I have seen a piercing knowledge that makes one know that nothing can be hidden from Him. My friend, I have seen a touch of sadness that somehow did not damper a sparkle of anticipation and joy shining in His eyes, eyes that reminded me of the joy of a lonely father who sees his prodigal children from afar and runs toward them to welcome them home.

I have written this book in love and in obedience to the words that have come to me from the still, small voice of God. Some of what is written may seem harsh, but keep in mind that some scriptures may also seem so. It is not my intention to placate or denigrate any specific church, creed, denomination, or personage; therefore, I will not use any identification of either church or location. When I write the word "church," I am referring to the entire living body of Christ from one end of the earth to the other!

God never sends warnings without also sending corresponding redeeming answers. God's Word is a double-edged sword: one edge cuts out the infection of sin, while the other edge heals and erases the scars.

If God's Word appears to be condemning, it is only because our own ornery spirits are battling with His Holy Spirit. God does not berate us; instead, we abuse ourselves when we resist His warnings. When an arrogant spirit continues on in this way unabated, it ultimately destroys itself. The humble spirit, on the other hand, welcomes the guiding hand.

——— ≪ **1** ≫ ———

TRANSFIGURATION

My UNEXPECTED JOURNEY to meet Jesus started in a hallway near the sanctuary of a church. While I was standing there, a woman whom I had always counted on as a trusted friend began pleading with me to attend one of these questionable types of meetings that had cropped up in a few churches in the 1960s. I had strongly opposed them, even called them cults, because they were being conducted in a manner that I thought bordered on hysteria.

While I did believe in both the indwelling of God's Spirit in the human heart and the gifts of the Spirit, as described in 1 Cor.12: 7–11, I also knew that Scripture clearly indicates that God distributes His gifts according to His will! In these meetings, people were demanding that God give them the gifts they wanted. This selfish approach did not take into consideration the fact that God does not give a specific gift to anyone that He knows cannot handle it wisely. Demanding the gift and not taking into consideration whether He wanted to give the gift added up to disobedience and disrespect for the will of God! When I had attended several of these types of meetings in the past, I had been concerned about the mental safety of the people. Most had been innocent people who did not understand enough of the Bible passages to know the error of what they were doing.

After the invitation, the woman told me that her group wanted to "save" me because I had "been possessed by the devil." They wanted to form a circle around me and pray that God would exorcise the evil spirit out of me. I quickly retorted, "No, it is you people who are the lost ones!" She took a step toward me, and I backed away. Then she said, "Betty, I love you. I'm worried for you. I don't want the devil to destroy you." She again moved toward me; and again, I moved away. Then she said, "Betty, listen to me, I love you and I just wanted to give you a kiss!" I said, "Yeah, and so did Judas betray Christ with a kiss!" With that, her jaw dropped, and I thought her eyes would come out of their sockets. It was as if I had hit her with a baseball bat.

I felt badly for her because I knew she was sincere and loved me. Love for her and for others like her had been the primary reason why I had taken such a strong stand against these groups. I am happy to say that by the grace of God these cult groups were short-lived.

After this incident, I grabbed my purse and ran out of the church. I drove safely home, but I can't remember how.

Sometimes the fact that we are all creatures of habit comes in handy. The car seemed to be on autopilot.

My husband was at work, and the children were still in school. Still shaken, I threw myself against the back of the couch and cried out, "God, why have I felt the danger so strongly against these cults, if they are not wrong? If it's me that's wrong, tell me. Please God, help me!"

Just as quickly as the inhaling and exhaling of one breath, I found myself somewhere else. I can understand what St. Paul meant when he said that in a twinkling of an eye, we would be changed. My body was still on the couch, but the part of me that is "me" was in a shadowy place. I was uneasy and felt utterly alone and abandoned. I called out, and then softly through the mist, my Savior Jesus came. Everything was so peaceful in His presence. I wanted to stay there with Him for-ever, but He told me that I had to go back. There was much He had destined me to accomplish for Him. Through me and my life, much glory, honor, and praise would be given to both Father and Son, and it would reach to the ends of the earth.

Jesus told me to never be distressed by the vicious, jealous, lying accusations that might come against me over the course of my lifetime. He assured me that I was not possessed by Satan, and would not be, because I was a beloved, obedient child of God, and He would never leave me. He told me not to be frightened or worried if people hated me, but to remember that they hated Him first.

Just that quickly, I was back in my living room and on the couch. This happened in 1964. I was thirty-seven years old. Shortly thereafter, I wrote the following poem, "Trans-figuration." In that same year, I also wrote a story, "Fact or Fantasy," which I will share in the next chapter. I would have other miraculous encounters in which the power of God was revealed to me, but none have so far been as traumatic and life-changing as the transfiguration.

I was completely puzzled by the things He had said to me during that first supernatural encounter. At the time, I could not understand how anything I wrote, even if the words and thoughts came from God, would reach to the ends of the earth. This was 1964, long before the use of computers became widespread. How could I have dreamed that the Internet and manmade satellites would make communication to the ends of the earth a real possibility for the average American?

When a prophecy comes from God, it is always fulfilled, even though it may be many years before it comes to fruition. When Jesus told me that my praise for both Father and Son would spread to the ends of the earth, He was actually telling me about the coming of the computer age. Because this kind of technology was way beyond my imagination, I could only receive His Words by faith and obey them. My testimony here points to the fact that He will do what He says He will do.

TRANSFIGURATION

> Deep in the vale of Morpheus,
> Between the mountains of twilight and dawn,
> I wandered lonelier than the dead God Zeus
> Through a life ne'er lived, yet is gone.
> Mythical Gods of earth are we,
> Our flesh devouring time;
> Hell-bent on gaining our place in the sun,
> Without reasoning or rhyme.
> Ruling transient kingdoms of material worth;
> Lost in clouds of intellect's dust.
> But there comes a day when we are forced to face
> The results of our misplaced trust.

Transfiguration

The swirling mist barely hid the black
Of the unknown path ahead,
Yet I had to go on, there was no turning back
To that life with the living dead.
Oh God, how my fainting soul did yearn
For just a place to rest.
It had reached the point of no return,
Gravely wounded within my breast.
How pitiful the harvest reaped from the world;
How stunted and bitter the fruit.
So insistent are we in sowing our seed,
In earth, where it cannot take root.

Was I all alone in this shadowy land;
Was there no one to share the grief
Of my wasted years, like grains of sand,
Washed up on a storm-swept reef?
Suddenly, a voice dispelled the gloom
As it gently called my name.
The stone rolled away from my self-sealed tomb,
As through mist my Savior came.
His deep-set eyes pierced my soul to the core;
I fell dying at His feet.
But, He raised me up with a cross of light,
And filled my heart with a strange new beat.

Vibrantly alive, I slipped away from myself,
With a wish to remain forever,
Suspended in peace at heaven's brink
Far removed from earth's endeavor.
But, He bade me return to my place in the world;
To walk where He would guide.
So, I lifted His cross; His glorious banner unfurled
And went forth with Christ by my side.
Oh, my Lord, how I long to help all my brothers
Know the joy of your presence within,

And to know that no one loves Jesus enough
To repay Him His death for our sin.

I do not expect to be numbered with saints,
Be their number ten thousand times seven,
But, Oh my Lord, I'd be content
Just to sweep the floors of heaven.
May my whole life sing with your song of praise,
And when my eyelids close in death,
May I murmur, "Oh Christ, I love you still,"
With my final flow of breath.
It matters not that His way may be hard,
Full of rejection; devoid of renown.
For the love of Christ is so compelling,
I cannot turn Him down!

—JUNE, 1965

2

FACT OR FANTASY?

HAVE YOU EVER had a dream you can't seem to forget? Well, I have, and it has bothered me so much that I want to pass it on to you. Maybe you can help me erase it by proving that there isn't any possibility that it could be true!

I dreamed that I had been away from my hometown for several years, and, upon my return to the city, the first thing I did was hurry to the church and the people I had loved so much from childhood on up. There she stood, strong and beautiful as ever. Her well-kept lawn, the steeple rising proudly into the sky, serene and untouched by the noise of traffic on the street. As I climbed the front steps, I became aware of a man standing to the side of the front doors. He smiled and came toward me. I noticed he was carrying an odd satchel. He said, "Pardon me, but would you allow me to go into the church with you? I have something to show you." I said, "Of course. Everyone is welcome here." A strange, sad look crossed his face as he replied, "No, my friend, everyone isn't welcome here. I have been coming here for years, but I get the distinct impression that I'm not really wanted inside."

Questions raced through my head as I wondered who he was, and why he said this. I answered, "You must be mistaken." He stood closer to me, and I was almost hypnotized by his magnificent eyes, the lines of care on his face, and the smile that came easily but never quite erased the sadness in his eyes. He said, "I'm a salesman, and I have the most wonderful products to sell that have ever been put on the market, but few will listen long enough to buy."

Just then, a woman rushed up the steps, bubbling over with energy and enthusiasm. The man approached her and said, "Excuse me, I wonder if I may have a moment of your time? I have important merchandise to show you." To that, the woman replied rather rudely, "I'm in a hurry—I don't have a minute to spare. All these last-minute things to do to get the church program whipped into shape." She rambled on, barely taking a breath, "You have no idea how much of my time is taken pulling all the loose ends together. But if I don't do it, it won't get done. Church work is so difficult that sometimes I'm a nervous wreck. Oh well, I'm sure I'll get my reward in heaven. God knows I've been a faithful servant all my life." With this, she flew past us into the building. The man slowly shook his head and said, "How little she knows of how much she really could do if only she would listen to me!"

We turned, as several cars pulled into the driveway, and

men climbed out of their cars and walked into the church. With a display of hope, the stranger started toward the men. He stopped one man and said, "May I talk to you a minute? I have something I'm sure would be of interest to you." The church man impatiently, but nevertheless politely, said, "Sorry sir, not now. A special council meeting has been called, and I don't want to be late and miss anything. Pretty important business is coming up, and as councilman, I'm charged with caring for the welfare of this church on behalf of the congregation. I take this service very seriously. It's my Christian responsibility not to let them down." He then turned and hurried away. The stranger looked at me and said, "If only he would have listened to me, he could have taken my products with him and fulfilled his office of obligation and trust to its fullest potential."

Suddenly, around the corner came a small child. She ran to the man and took his hand. "Hi, mister," she said.

A warm smile lighted his face as he said, "Well, hello there, Suzie. How are you today?" Suzie giggled and said, "Oh, I'm fine, and I came to help you pull weeds around the flowers."

The child's mother came toward us and said, "Oh, there you are. Come on, we'll be late for Sunday school."

"But Mommy," Suzie protested, "I promised my friend I'd help him work on the lawn. He comes here every day and takes care of our church. He can do anything."

The woman grabbed her hand and exclaimed, "Suzie, don't you dare get dirty! I've spent hours washing and ironing your clothes. You can't go into God's house looking like a little ragamuffin. Come now, Mama knows best."

The child turned, disappointment showing plainly in her voice as she said, "Sorry mister, I gotta go now, but someday when Mommy isn't looking, I'll be back to work for you."

The stranger smiled knowingly, and said, "Yes, child, I believe you will."

The more encounters I witnessed in this dream, the more puzzled I became, for the people had no faces. I asked him, "Haven't you gone inside our church in all the years you've been coming here?" "Yes," he replied, "A few times, with various individuals who thought it was their Christian duty to invite a visitor to worship with them. They sat me in a corner and told me not to disturb anybody when I tried to tell them about the items in my satchel. They walked away, completely serene in the thought that they had done a good deed. They didn't care that I felt rejected. They can't comprehend another's needs, much less their own, because they are so wrapped up in this outward facade of Christian behavior. So, I got up and left. Most people didn't know I was there, and no one at all was aware that I had gone!"

By now, words were literally tumbling out of my mouth. "Well, I just do not understand this. Have you spoken to our pastor about it? I'm sure he wouldn't allow anyone to treat you like this." The man's eyes shone with understanding as he said, "Oh, yes, he knows I'm here. As a matter of fact, he constantly opens the doors for me, but before I can step in, people seem to come from nowhere and slam the door shut."

More questions bubbled forth. "Well, why do you stay here and suffer this humiliation and rejection? Can't you find another market for your products? What, by the way, are you selling?" The man laughed out loud, then quickly became serious when he answered, "Yes, I can and do sell a lot better out in the highways and hedges, because there are people out there who are searching for a new life. But it's the church people who have my concern. They need my wares desperately. You see, they blindly, but sincerely, think

14

they already have everything they could possibly need."

The man quickly opened his satchel, displaying three packages while he said, "I'm glad you asked what I was selling." One of the items was a loaf of bread, one was a bottle of unidentifiable liquid, and the third was a pair of eyeglasses. As the stranger offered the spectacles to me, he said, "Here, try these on. Don't be afraid if they hurt your eyes. The lenses are very strong. Some people can't wear them at all because they are too painful, but if you can take it for a little while, then the discomfort will wear off and you will see everything differently." I thought to myself that anything so powerful and unique must cost a fortune. The stranger read my thoughts, for he said, "There's no money involved, but the price I ask may be more than you will want to pay—for it means giving up everything that is so important in your earthbound life. My price is that you give me yourself."

After these successive statements, I was more than a little bewildered. I blurted out, "What kind of a nutcase are you? No wonder no one would let you in." But the unspoken pleading in the man's eyes compelled me to listen when he said, "Please try on these glasses. If you can't stand them, take them off. Most people do." So, I put them on. He was right! They caused excruciating pain, but after the initial shock waves subsided, my vision cleared and I saw beauty beyond anything my poor mind previously could have conceived. The world took on a new glow, and I could even hear the music of heaven. The skies opened up, and I felt as though I were a part of the whole universe; a part of the very force of life itself!

I saw my church, not as she had been in the past, but as what she could become. Not a carefully sheltered citadel, unperturbed by anything happening around her. Rather, she became a great beacon whose rays spread the light of hope and truth into every dark corner of the world. She became the true church, whose members retained their individual identities but functioned miraculously as the living body of Christ!

What had looked like an ordinary loaf of bread became flesh with a heartbeat, and the bottle of liquid became the lifeblood of Jesus Christ, red and flowing. For the first time, I felt the impact of the communion sacrament rather than just mouthing mere words about it. I experienced the sensation of the saving grace of God that was given to mankind at the most hideous price anyone could be asked to pay—the life of His only Son! I was overwhelmed with shame as I thought of how many times I, as well as many others, had taken this costly gift for granted and given little more than lip-service in return.

It suddenly dawned on me that these glasses made me look at things through God's eyes. No wonder the stranger warned me that they would hurt. At that moment I was glad there were no mirrors around. The agony of looking at myself through God's eyes might have been more than I could bear. I turned to look at the salesman, and a choking scream woke me up as it rose into my throat! The stranger was Jesus Christ!

I shuddered as I murmured a half-prayer, half-sigh of relief, "Thank God, this was only a dream." Yet an uncanny sense of foreboding remained with me. I could still see those magnificent, compelling eyes of the Man outside our church, and I began to wonder what if this were not a dream, but the stark reality of truth. I couldn't face truth in broad daylight, so I dismissed it as a dream. Then an even more troublesome thought came to me: what if this were indeed fact and not fantasy? And if so, even though the love and patience of the Son of God is beyond human understanding, how much longer can we expect to get away with slamming the door in Christ's face?

—1965

AN INTERMISSION

The space between what God compelled me to write in the 1960s and my reawakening to write again in 2000 was thirty-five years. The messages I received after the transfiguration seemed to be God's way of opening the door, just a crack, to reveal a much-needed view of a higher spiritual level.

The staid, stodgy, prim, and proper façade of Christian behavior was all that religion meant to most people in the 1960s, and they were not ready to accept the exploding light caused by the appearance of the Holy Spirit in the human heart. Hate and jealousy took over too many. There were no vicious, gossiping, lying, scandalous accusations that were not leveled against me. I found myself *almost* wanting to hate them back, but I cannot live with either hate or unforgiveness. The time had come to "shake the dust from my feet" and move on (Mark 6:11). Our family and I took our letters of membership and transferred them to a small church in the suburbs. My husband's health was continuing to deteriorate, and we did not attend church regularly at that time. I believe that God was also giving me time to heal. I came out of that time of testing wiser and stronger than I had ever been before because God's guiding hand never left me. I held my head high and kept going! God gave me *vision* to see beyond my circumstances!

During this time I had the responsibility of looking to the needs of my aged grandmother, a mother whose health was failing, and a sister who was dying. Along with all this, my husband had the first of four heart attacks and my oldest son was sent to Vietnam three times while serving in a construction unit with the Navy Sea-Bees. I struggled to keep our lifestyle on an even keel so the three children still living at home would not become frightened.

At times I was so tired, so nervous, and yes, even angry and fed-up with my situation that I thought I could not take another step. Then came the realization that I had to, hypothetically, dump all my cares, all my responsibilities, and all my frustrations into a huge wash basket filled with all the "dirty linen" that life throws at us. I took hold of one of the handles, and Christ took hold of the other! Together, we carried the load and emerged victorious. My grandmother, my mother, my sister, and my husband had gone home to be with the Lord by 1978.

During those remaining years until my retirement, I worked at a job that I loved and was free to study Scripture in depth, with the Holy Spirit as my guide and my teacher. My testimony is about a loving, loyal Savior who never abandons His children. He didn't just die for us, He lives for us, and He carries us on His shoulders when the mud of our lives gets too thick and too deep.

———— ≪ 3 ≫ ————

THE HUMAN HEART:
THE MATRIX
OF THE HOLY SPIRIT

In those days Caesar Augustus issued a decree that a census should be taken of the entire Roman world....So Joseph also went up from the town of Nazareth in Galilee to Judea, to Bethlehem the town of David...He went there to register with Mary, who was pledged to be married to him and was expecting a child. While they were there, the time came for the baby to be born, and she gave birth to her firstborn, a son. She wrapped him in cloths and placed him in a manger, because there was no place for them in the inn.

—Luke 2:1, 4–7

A ND THERE WAS no place for them in the inn" was a precursor, a sign, or, if you will, a prophecy of what our beloved Savior would face during His life on earth. The reading of the biblical account of Jesus' life among men shows that this indeed was what He faced while He was on earth. However, two thousand years later it is still the case.

Even in His hometown of Nazareth, He was ridiculed and rejected. This gave evidence of the truth of the scripture, "I tell you the truth, no prophet is accepted in his hometown" (Luke 4:24). The more Jesus spoke the truth and wisdom of God's Word, the angrier the people in the synagogue became, "and they took him to the brow of the hill on which the town was built, in order to throw him down the cliff. But he walked right through the crowd and went on his way" (Luke 4: 29–30). Jesus never again returned to Nazareth.

This beautiful man who was born of a virgin, the God-head incarnate, was treated like dirt by those He had created out of dirt. He was, and still is, being rejected by those for whom He was born to give the chance of redemption from eternal death.

"We all, like sheep, have gone astray, each of us has turned to his own way; and the Lord has laid on Him the iniquity of us all. He was oppressed and afflicted, yet he did not open his mouth; he was led like a lamb to the slaughter, and as a sheep before her shearers is silent, so he did not open his mouth" (Isa. 53:6–7).

The scripture above describes what Christ faced during His first visit to earth. But today things are different! He has already "been there, done that!" Now, the voice of the Lamb will not be silenced!

Jesus came, by the power of the love of God, so that we would not remain just flesh and bones filled with the breath of life, breathed upon us by our Creator. Jesus came so that we could become a rejuvenated copy of the glorious body of our resurrected Lord! Having finished this redemptive work of the cross and the Resurrection, He waits with joyous anticipation of greeting those whose hearts belong to Him.

The human heart; the matrix of the Holy Spirit! According to Webster's Dictionary, the word matrix is defined as "that within which something originates, or takes form." The seed of the Holy Spirit was given to the world as Jesus gasped His last breaths on the cross and said, "It is finished!" "When he had received the [vinegar], Jesus said, 'It is finished.' With that, he bowed his head and gave up his spirit" (John 19:30).

The fulfillment of our spiritual destiny has just begun when the concept, or reality, of the Holy Spirit is introduced into the human heart. This awakening of the Spirit within us is just the beginning of a more exquisite cognizance of the eternal dimension to which we are called by God. If the spiritual awakening never grows beyond a microscopic fetal stage because it is not being fed and nourished by the wisdom of God's Holy Word, it can wither and die on the vine.

Many people call themselves "born-again" Christians because they have "felt" a spiritual shiver. They do not have the foggiest notion that is takes time to produce a heavenly birth; that they must journey from level to level, from glory to glory, before a full-term spiritual baby is born! Hunger and thirst for the righteousness of God speeds up the process dramatically, especially if it is combined with the belief that God is always with us and ready to pick us up if we fall and skin our knees.

Most people today do not realize that God is a jealous God! The first of the Ten Commandments is, "Thou shalt have no other gods before me" (Exod. 20:3, KJV). The "gods" or idols of western society may not be as easy to identify as a statue that one kneels before in worship. However, anything that divides our hearts from God, that takes precedence over our relationship with God, is a "god." A half-hearted relationship with God is similar to a condominium that has a soundproof wall dividing the living space in half. In my analogy, one half of the condo (or our heart) is dedicated to the fulfillment of our selfish desires and building up our egos, while the other half is where we fulfill what we perceive to be our religious duties. Allowing the religious duty half to overtake the selfish desires and ego part would not be enough. In fact, that would actually be a form of religious legalism because the "works" are not born out of a whole-hearted personal relationship with God.

From this illustration, we can see that a half-hearted relationship with God is actually no relationship at all. This is because God will only be satisfied with being first place in our hearts, with all of our priorities being subjected to His. In this, God reigns over and is the very fabric of our whole heart. When God is ruler over our whole heart, every aspect of our lives is His dwelling place. When we lay our idols at His feet, He gives back full measure, running over. The mansions, or eternal homes, that Jesus promised He has prepared for those who love and follow Him are beyond any finite home we could ever dream about. Any earthly palace or mansion are but shacks when compared to the numerous and incomprehensible expressions of His love for us here on earth and in heaven.

> Is your heart just an Inn with no room to spare,
> or with pangs of conscience,
> you offer Him the shed at the back of your property?
>
> Is your heart merely a condominium, with sound-
>   proof walls separating your
> life from God's life – but you give Him the other half
>   of the space just in
> case there's an emergency, and you might need Him?
>
> Or, is your heart the Presidential Suite, reserved exclu-
>   sively for Jesus Christ,
> the King of Kings, the Lord of lords, and the Alpha
>   and Omega?

Jesus is the love of God Himself! He is the Prince of Peace that passeth all understanding!

—— **A PRAYER** ——

Lord God, all praise, honor, and glory belong to You. I want my whole heart and life to be Your dwelling place. Please show me any idols in my heart that are separating me from You, and please show me how to tear them down. In the name of the Prince of Peace, Jesus Christ, I pray. Amen.

---— ≪ **4** ≫ ---—

WISDOM = UNDERSTANDING = VISION

"This is what he used to teach me, "Let your heart treasure what I have to say; keep my principles and you will live; acquire wisdom, acquire understanding, never forget her, never deviate from my words. Do not desert her, she will keep you safe; love her she will watch over you. The first principle of wisdom is; acquire wisdom at the cost of all you have; acquire understanding; embrace her and she will be your pride!"

—Proverbs 29:4–8, New Jerusalem Bible

"Where there is no vision, the people perish!"

—Proverbs 29:18, kjv

THE NUMBER OF people who are unaware that more than going to church is required for entrance into the kingdom of heaven is the reason why the overall church, worldwide, is fundamentally weak. While pastors are toning down their messages in order to avoid offending anyone lest the attendance roles shrink, they are doing a grave disservice to those people who are in for an irrevocable shock when they come face to face with God and hear Him say, "Depart from me, I never knew you."

"Many will say to me in that day, Lord, Lord, have we not prophesied in thy name? and in thy name have cast out devils?

and in thy name done many wonderful works? And then will I profess unto them, I never knew you: depart from me, ye that work iniquity" (Matt. 7:22–23, KJV). For those people who have not been told that there is room at the cross for them, the tragedy will be eternal if they are not made aware of the fullness of the gospel.

The fault of the error does not fall squarely on pastors who fail to give warning and point to the imperative need for us to surrender all. The fault also lies with the vast majority of people who have bought into the self-centered consumeristic perspective of life that is so prevalent in western cultures today. This expectation of instant gratification at the least cost possible may also be seen in the fact that we want forgiveness of sin, eternal life, the mansions He has prepared for us, peace, our bodies healed…our prayers answered. We want, we want, we want—with little or no regard for the fact that He has already given us far more than we deserve. All too often, we are so consumed with figuring out what more we can get God to give us that we completely overlook the fact that in receiving eternal life in Jesus Christ, we exchange death for life, our life for His. When He creates in us a new spirit and a new heart that beats only for Him, our eye will be on Him rather than on what He might give us.

While God does invite us to come to Him just as we are, this does not mean that we are to remain just as we are. Saying a few contrite words is not enough. Change in conduct is also necessary. For example, God can even forgive a murderer, but God would not share His kingdom with a man who said a contrite prayer but continued murdering people. The same concept applies to other types of sin, whether seemingly small or seemingly large. Only God can accomplish the change in us that is required.

The Bible is much more than an history or geography book. It is the living Word of God that unveils God's redemptive plan for us. For us to understand His Word, we must be born of the Spirit of God. This is because His Word is Spirit, and when we are born of the Spirit, we understand the things of the Spirit. When the Holy Spirit dwells in us, we receive wisdom and understanding from God because our vision is no longer darkened by our former state of spiritual death. "Where there is no vision, the people perish" (Prov. 29:18, KJV). The New International Version phrases the scripture: "Where there is no revelation, the people cast off restraint."

Even after salvation, our vision may be blurred by false suppositions that creep into our interpretation of Scripture. One such falsehood is sometimes referred to as liberal Christian theology. This deception denies even the most fundamental elements of Scripture that relate to God's plan for the redemption of mankind. The denial of the downfall of mankind through the disobedience of Adam and Eve and the denial of the resurrection of Jesus Christ is a denial of man's need for redemption and the only way in which that may be accomplished. Rejection of scriptural declarations that Jesus is the Son of God who was born of a virgin also are deceptions that deny God's plan for mankind, not to mention blasphemous.

In His Word, God warns us that there will be false prophets and teachings based upon misinterpretations of Scripture. One example is: "But there were also false prophets among the people, just as there will be false teachers among you. They will secretly introduce destructive heresies, even denying the sovereign Lord who bought them—bringing swift destruction on themselves. Many will follow their shameful ways and will bring the way of truth into disrepute. In their greed these teachers will exploit you with stories they have made up. Their condemnation has long been hanging over them, and their destruction has not been sleeping" (2 Pet. 2:1–3).

As we see the myths that contradict scriptures blasted over the airways and in every other form of media, we can remain confident in God's assurance that "Heaven and earth will pass away, but my words will never pass away" (Matt. 24:35).

Going to church or saying a little prayer does not add up to spending eternity with the Lord in heaven, if not coupled with having Jesus Christ as our live-in companion. And even then, we must guard our hearts and minds against those teachings that oppose the truth of God's Word. "For false Christs and false prophets will appear and perform great signs and miracles to deceive the elect—if that were possible. See, I have told you ahead of time" (Matt. 24:24–25).

—— A PRAYER ——

Dear God, help me to seek Your wisdom and find Your depth of understanding, and not deviate from your eternal Word. Give me the vision to see things the way that You see them and to quickly recognize all philosophies and teachings that oppose Your Word. In Jesus Christ's holy name, I pray. Amen

—— ≪≪ 5 ≫≫ ——

GOD'S GIFT OF JOY
AND LAUGHTER

Gladness of heart is life to anyone, joy is what gives
length of days.
—ECCLESIASTICUS 30:22, NEW JERUSALEM BIBLE

B ECAUSE THE PHRASE "Laughter is the best medicine"
is an old saying, we may tend to dismiss it as a mundane
idiom. However, the Bible refers many times to the benefits of
having a heart that is filled with joy and gladness. Laughter is
one expression of joy. Another expression is God's people displaying their love and worship of God through joyous song,
dance, clapping, or playing of musical instruments.

Meditating on the goodness of God is one sure way to
bring joy and merriment to our hearts. By His goodness and
love, God not only gave us the chance to be forgiven and
redeemed through the sacrifice of his Son, but He set us free

to experience such gladness of heart that we can laugh without having the inhibition of being weighted down by sin.

A sense of humor and the ability to chuckle at our own human idiosyncrasies is a precious gift. Our lightheartedness does not mean that we are taking our Savior's sacrifice for granted or think that repentance and obedience is a laughing matter. However, when our love for Him awakens His spirit within us, then we quite naturally are set free to laugh, clap our hands, dance with joy, and sing out about what is in our hearts. Jesus said that He came so that we might have life in abundance: "I am come that they might have life, and that they might have it more abundantly" (John 10:10, KJV).

Observe the living "happiness" that exists around us. Observe the graceful dancing and swaying of the leaves when the gentle music of a breeze passes through the trees. Listen to the songs of the birds, their little throats and chests almost bursting with joy as they worship their maker—just so happy to be alive. Watch a little stream bounce with childish delight over the rocks. Cherish the colors, beauty, and perfection of every kind of flower with their faces always turned upward in unashamed adoration of God. Drink in the shading and hues of a brilliant sunset our Creator paints, and which no artist can duplicate. Feel the breathtaking grandeur of a snow-capped mountain as it reaches up to kiss the edge of heaven. God's magnificent genius lives all around us!

I have always been acutely aware of the presence and touch of God in all nature. Writing of the splendor of God's creation reminds me of a poem I wrote in 1942 as an assignment for my English Literature class. Comparing the thoughts I wrote down when I was 15 with those I have expressed here show that my love and wonder for God began when I was a child and has continued on. I believe I was meant to give praise, honor, and glory to God before I was ever born.

THE VOICE OF ETERNITY

As I sat on the cliff above the sea
Watching the whitecaps wriggle with glee;
Watching the seagulls gracefully soar,
Happy with freedom – wanting nothing more.

The waters stretched to horizon's end,
Where earth and sky seemed to magically blend.
Then a peace I had never known before
Encompassed me, and my space of shore.

The real meaning of life began to unfold;
Life not harried by desires for Gold,
And all the cares that had troubled my day,
Passed into nothingness – so far away.

The chains of my self-made bondage were broken.
The voice of eternity had softly spoken.
How small the minds of men can be;
How blind and deaf and dumb are we.

We scramble blindly for earthy gain,
Ignoring God's free gifts, and asking for pain.
For, long after man's poor efforts cease,
God and His universe will go on in peace!

—1942

If we would just take time to observe the splendor of God's creation and to ponder what is available to us through Jesus Christ during our lives here on earth, our joy would be much fuller. We could even enter into the place of joy unspeakable when we also look toward God's promise that a new heaven, new earth, and new Jerusalem will come down from above and when we begin to grasp that all will then be new, eternally beautiful, and wholly perfect! "Then I saw a new heaven and a new earth, for the first heaven and the first earth had passed away, and there was no longer any sea. I saw the Holy City, the new Jerusalem, coming down out of heaven from God, prepared as a bride beautifully dressed for her husband" (Rev. 21:1–2).

—— **A PRAYER** ——

Dear God, help my joy and laughter to rise as incense to heaven, giving all praise, honor, and glory to You. I thank You that Jesus Christ lives in the gladness of my heart. In Jesus's name, I pray. Amen

—❦ 6 ❧—

PORTRAIT OF
A 21ST CENTURY PHARISEE

But the Lord said to him, "You Pharisees! You clean the
outside of the cup and plate, while inside yourselves you
are filled with extortion and wickedness. Fools!"
—LUKE 11:39, 40, NEW JERUSALEM BIBLE

Alas for you Pharisees, because you like to take the seats
of honour in the synagogues and to be greeted respect-
fully in the market squares! Alas for you, because you
are like the unmarked tombs that people walk on without knowing it!
—LUKE 11:43–44 NEW JERUSALEM BIBLE

DURING JESUS' TIME He dealt with the Pharisees of
His day. Today, we are dealing with the Pharisees of our day.
By this I mean that in churches today there are still people
cleaving to their own definitions of holiness while inflicting
arrogant self-righteousness upon others. A modern-day Pharisee seldom is alone. Instead, a group of judgmental folks feed
one another and intimidate others into giving them seats of
power in the church.

Their power may not be because of position, but they
often run the church behind the scenes through the threat
of loss of income to the church if they were to leave and take

their tithes elsewhere. They also may be privy to information that they hold over leader's heads. They also probably have set themselves up as being seemingly indispensable because they have not left room for anyone else to be of assistance to church leaders in matters of importance. This does not mean that everyone active in the church is a type of Pharisee, but Christians must be on guard against those who would set themselves up in positions of power through intimidation, fear, and judgments that are based on unbalanced doctrine.

The loving, loyal ones who quietly do God's will without expectation of praise are those who are portraying the character of God and his true church. Their service is motivated by love, not the possibility of elevation to importance! Their focus is on doing for the gospel's sake rather than on telling others what to do.

> Be on your guard against the yeast of the Pharisees—their hypocrisy. Everything now covered up will be uncovered, and everything now hidden will be made clear. For this reason, whatever you have said in the dark will be heard in the daylight, and what you have whispered in hidden places will be proclaimed from the housetops.
> —Luke 12:1–3, New Jerusalem Bible

Would God accept a Pharisee who humbly and sincerely comes to Him? Yes, of course. God's heart is open to all! It is not His wish that any be lost! However, this is no more likely to happen today than it did in Christ's time on earth because they think that their sins are so small that they do not need to repent or ask for forgiveness. Again, we are brought to the fact that God's Word must be the basis from which we live. If not, we might get caught up in yet another false doctrine—the opinions of men or women who have not had their motives or doctrines straightened out by God's Word and Spirit.

In order not to be manipulated into taking on the mindsets and ways of the Pharisee, we must not be fooled by the pretense of humility. First off, we must be checking our own motives constantly. And secondly, we must be "wise as serpents, and harmless as doves" (Matt. 10:16, KJV). We cannot harm, or wish to harm, anyone. But, we must walk in wisdom so as not to be fooled, or led astray, by those who would harm us or harm others. Like in Jesus' day, one tactic of the Pharisee is gossip, to incite accusation against the body of Christ. By walking in truth and by God's Spirit, we will see ways in which we might ward off such attacks against those who are just beginning to awaken and grow into Spirit-filled faith. We have particular responsibility to protect newborns from the poison of negative attitudes that would repel them from the protection of the family of God.

—— **A PRAYER** ——

Dear God, rescue us from all the negative aspects that Satan tries to slip into the church through unwanted criticism. Wake us up and give us the strength of Holy Spirit power to accentuate all the positive blessings of your love and encouragement, not only in Christ's body, but also to project it outwardly into a world that is desperately in need of a transfusion from the redeeming blood of Christ. We give You and Your beloved Son all praise, honor, and glory. In His name we pray. Amen.

—— ⋘ 7 ⋙ ——

THE DEVIL, DEATH, AND DUST

> Then shall the dust return to the earth as it was: and the spirit shall return unto God who gave it. Vanity of vanities, saith the preacher; all is vanity.
>
> —ECCLESIASTES 12:7–8, KJV

TO ME, THIS is one of the most profound passages of Scripture. None of the frantic efforts to climb the ladder of success, or to keep up with the Joneses, or to see our names in the neon lights of Broadway, or to cram our limited cranial cavities with meaningless trivia, or to pile up massive amounts of assets will edify the true church or lead a lost soul to Christ. In summation, anything without eternal value is but vanity.

Why, then, are we here? In love, God placed us on this beautiful planet called earth to love and care for it, but most of all, to care for each other. Earth is the place where we are given the opportunity to follow the pathway that leads back to Him! Will we accept the indwelling of the Holy Spirit that will bring us new life? Or will we be so obsessed with vanity that we miss our appointment to receive Christ?

In the Garden of Eden God gave mankind free will. There, Adam and Eve, who personified mankind, were beautifully protected and provided for. There, Adam and Eve, used their free will to choose vanity over obedience to God.

Even though they had chosen vanity over Him, God's love did not fail there. Right then and there, He initiated His plan to redeem mankind. God is pure love, so profound that He decided to send His beloved Son, Jesus Christ, into the world as the *last chance* for the souls of the inhabitants of the earth to find their way back to our Creator!

In God's plan to redeem us back to Himself, if we surrender the vanity of our lives without Christ, all that is of true value will be added unto us. He gives us new eyes to see the beauty of our lives and a new love with which to touch the lives of others. Because we walk in the Spirit, we live in the world but we are not of the world. In other words, we march to the beat of a different drum—Christ's drum, that is. "Now we have received, not the spirit of the world, but the spirit which is of God; that we might know the things that are freely given to us of God" (1 Cor. 2:12, KJV).

When we are Christ's, we point others to Jesus rather than vainly trying to draw attention to ourselves.

> Let him who boasts, boast of the Lord. For it is not the man who commends himself that is accepted, but the man whom the Lord commends.
> —2 CORINTHIANS 10:17–18, RSV

> Everything they do is done for men to see.
> —MATTHEW 23:5

We can't have the indwelling of the Holy Spirit without manifesting "good works." But we can do "good works" without accepting God's Spirit into our hearts. How many people have wasted precious time proudly boasting about how much they have done and do for the church? In some cases, they know much about God but do not actually know Him. Unfortunately, the church is just the environment in which they are chasing after vanity. The difference between the true servant and those that use the church environment as a platform from which to boast is a matter of whether the heart is after God or the vanity of this world.

God warns the inhabitants of the earth to love His Son. Because God loves his Son, He only invites those who are of His Son to spend eternal life in fellowship with Him. Whether we love the Son or love the vanity of this world more will be reflected in the choice we make.

The span of time of our life on this earth is so fleeting. We are like the petals on a flower that drop off the stem and return to dust. However, even though life is so short, people waste their time on earth here even though they are offered the opportunity to contribute to what is everlasting.

Unlike the endeavors of vanity, we do not have to struggle to get Christ's attention. All we need to do is sincerely confess our sins, turn from our sin, and confess that He is our Lord and Savior. When we open the door of our heart to Jesus Christ, we have opened ourselves up to receive the love of God. "That Christ may dwell in your hearts by faith; that ye, being rooted and grounded in love, may be able to comprehend with all saints what is the breadth, and length, and depth, and height; and to know the love of Christ, which passeth knowledge, that ye might be filled with all the fulness of God" (Eph. 3:17–19, KJV).

Receiving Jesus into our hearts is just the beginning of our love relationship with Him. By faith, we are rooted and grounded in that love and, over time, comprehend the span of His love. Only by the Holy Spirit can we know the richness of His love, the love that is beyond human understanding. Through the Holy Spirit-given comprehension of that love, we may be filled with all the fullness of God. Any motivation outside of receiving, comprehending, and expressing God's love is vanity. Why settle for anything less?

—— **A Prayer** ——

Dear God, open my eyes and my heart so that I may see any areas of my life where vanity still has a grip on me. Help me to comprehend the breadth, length, depth, and height of Your love so that I can receive and give that love. Thank You for making a way for us to have a love relationship with You. In Jesus Christ's name, I pray. Amen.

8

WHERE IS
THE KINGDOM OF GOD?

But seek first his kingdom and his righteousness, and all things will be given to you as well. Therefore do not worry about tomorrow, for tomorrow will worry about itself.

—MATTHEW 6:33–34

"The kingdom of God does not come with your careful observation, nor will people say, 'Here it is,' or 'There it is,' because the kingdom of God is within you."

—LUKE 17:20–21

"THE KINGDOM OF God is here, and it's now! If we do not find His kingdom while we are still on this earth, then we cannot expect to find "pie in the sky when we die." The kingdom of God, literally, is the acceptance of the indwelling of the Holy Spirit in our hearts. From the very first flutter of the awakening of His Spirit within us—like the very first, feeble, fluttering movement of an unborn child in the womb, we can grow into the fully developed stature and strength of a mature soldier of Christ. When we are born again in the Spirit, we are to put on the full armor of God so that we withstand attacks from Satan and deflect attacks aimed at others.

"Finally, be strong in the Lord and in his mighty power. Put on the full armor of God so that you can take your stand against the devil's schemes. For our struggle is not against flesh and blood, but against the rulers, against the authorities, against the powers of this dark world and against the spiritual forces of evil in the heavenly realms" (Eph. 6:10–12).

Because we are in God's care and wear His armor, we need not be afraid of what tomorrow may bring. "Surely God is my salvation; I will trust and not be afraid. The Lord, the Lord, is my strength and my song; he has become my salvation" (Isa. 12:2).

A contemporary form of satanic attack is the fear and threat that he has brought through terrorists. I believe that in spite of America's spiritual failings, God's love for her has not failed. Our safety as a nation will return through trusting in God and wearing the full armor of God. Along with this, we must never turn against Israel, for God blesses the nation that blesses Israel and curses the nation that curses Israel.

On a personal level, trusting in God and always having on the full armor of God will enable us to withstand and thwart satanic attacks. While we live in the peace of God, we must at the same time remain on guard against the wiles of the enemy of our own souls. We must live like the authority of the kingdom of God is within us, not in some far away place.

> When the hand of Jesus touches you,
> You will never be the same.
> When the hand of Jesus touches you,
> You will truly know His name.
> When the hand of Jesus touches you,
> You can throw aside sin's shame.
> When the hand of Jesus touches you,
> You will know just why He came.

When the eyes of Jesus look into yours,
You will grasp a life that's new.
When the eyes of Jesus look into yours,
You will catch a heavenly view.
When the eyes of Jesus look into yours,
You will feel your heart beat anew.
When the eyes of Jesus look into yours,
You will melt before your Savior true.

When the heart of Jesus beats along with yours,
You will know indescribable peace.
When the heart of Jesus beats along with yours,
Your praise for God will never cease.
When the heart of Jesus beats along with yours,
Your love for others will increase.
When the heart of Jesus beats along with yours,
Your soul will find sweet release.

When the touch and heartbeat of Christ is your goal,
And you invite Him to dwell within your soul.
You will never want for anything more,
For He fills all needs to the very core.
Oh, my Jesus, how could anyone turn you away,
When your death was such a horrible price to pay?
Oh, my Jesus, take my life to use as you will,
And may my song of praise, the heavens fill!

—— A PRAYER ——

Oh, God, how can we ever repay You, or prove how sorry we are that a love like Yours cost you the life of Your only Child? Help us to have a "garage sale of the soul" and get rid of all the narcissistic things that clutter our lives, leaving little room for Christ. We pray in Jesus' name that His suffering was not in vain! Amen.

WISDOM'S CALL

To you, O men, I (wisdom) call out; I raise my voice to all mankind. You who are simple, gain prudence; you who are foolish, gain understanding. Listen for I have worthy things to say; I open my lips to speak what is right. My mouth speaks what is true, for my lips detest wickedness. All the words of my mouth are just; none of them is crooked or perverse. To the discerning, all of them are right; they are faultless to those who have knowledge. Choose my instruction instead of silver, knowledge rather than choice gold, for wisdom is more precious than rubies, and nothing you desire can compare with her. By me kings reign and rulers make laws that are just; by me princes govern, and all nobles who rule on earth. I love those who love me, and those who seek me, find me.

—PROVERBS 8:4–11, 15–17

I N THE SCRIPTURE above, wisdom is calling to us. Wisdom and knowledge comes through the Word of God. Without them, we dwell:

Deep in the vale of Morpheus,
Between the mountains of twilight and dawn.
We wander lonelier than the dead God Zeus,
Through a life ne'er lived, yet is gone.
Mythical gods of earth are we,
Our flesh devouring time;

Hell-bent on gaining our place in the sun,
Without reasoning or rhyme.
Ruling transient kingdoms of material worth;
Lost in clouds of intellect's dust.
But there comes a day we are forced to face
The results of our misplaced trust.

Without wisdom, we are walking in the lull of deception. In other words, we are wide-awake sleepwalkers, spending most of our spiritual lives asleep while living our mortal lives thinking that we have all there is to want. Our wake-up call is described in the last lines of the poem, which represent the beginning of wisdom. The day we realize that we will remain dead if we do not live by the Word of God is the day of our wake-up call. Some will respond to the call by choosing the abundance of life that is only available through Jesus Christ, the Word of God who became flesh for us. Others will reject the call and choose to return to the apathy of spiritual blindness and eternal death.

In Proverbs 8:15–17, wisdom is crying out to the governors of nations. It is easy to see that America's government leaders have not heeded that cry well. To see this, we only have to consider the wide acceptance of witchcraft, cult religions, atheism, pornography, and the like that are protected under a perverted interpretation of our Bill of Rights; or one can examine how these same perverted interpretations of the Bill of Rights are being used to ban the Christian words "God," "Jesus," and the "Bible" from most elements of American public life.

Because Jesus is the Word of God that was made flesh for us, a nation that casts out God's Word from its society also is casting out Jesus Christ. This is very dangerous because in so doing it is casting out the avenue through which God expresses His grace and His love.

When Jesus Christ returns to earth, this time He will come with a fierce countenance: "And I saw heaven opened, and behold a white horse; and he that sat upon him was called Faithful and True, and in righteousness he doth judge and make war. His eyes were as a flame of fire, and on his head were many crowns; and he had a name written, that no man knew, but he himself. And he was clothed with a vesture dipped in blood: and his name is called The Word of God. And the armies which were in heaven followed him upon white horses, clothed in fine linen, white and clean. And out of his mouth goeth a sharp sword, that with it he should smite the nations: and he shall rule them with a rod of iron: and he treadeth the winepress of the fierceness and wrath of Almighty God. And he hath on his vesture and on his thigh a name written, KING OF KINGS, AND LORD OF LORDS" (Rev. 19:11–16, KJV).

Wisdom is crying out to the nations of the world, "Kiss the Son, lest he be angry, and ye perish from the way, when his wrath is kindled but a little. Blessed are all they that put their trust in him" (Ps. 2:12, KJV).

Wisdom is crying out to individuals and to nations. The voice of the Lamb will not be silenced.

One-half cup of self-satisfied, lukewarm faith, mixed with one-half cup of fear, is the recipe for a lethal drink, for which there is only one antidote that can reverse the effects of this kind of poison! Drink of the "living water" found in the Word of God. Take and eat of the body of Christ. Drink the blood, which was shed for you, and you will never hunger or thirst again, nor can any of the world's poison kill you.

——— A Prayer ———

Dear God, please put your spotlight of truth on the deception that so permeates American society today. Please open the eyes of America's government leaders to Your truth and to the need to put Your Word at the center of every decision. Lord, please have mercy on America and on the nations of the world. In Jesus Christ's holy name, I pray. Amen

⸺ ❦ 10 ❦ ⸺

STAY IN THE RACE TO THE END!

I have fought the good fight to the end; I have run the race to the finish; I have kept the faith; all there is to come for me now is the crown of uprightness which the Lord, the upright judge, will give to me on that Day; and not only to me but to all those who have longed for his appearing.

—2 Timothy 4:7–8, New Jerusalem Bible

St. Paul wrote those words of scripture above shortly before he was taken from the prison in Rome and beheaded somewhere along the Appian Way. A triumphant victory of a life in Jesus Christ that has been run without fainting or faltering has three undeniable characteristics: endurance, fire, and steadfastness. Each of these is essential to victory over the snares or stumbling blocks that Satan may place in our path to stop us.

Endurance does not necessarily mean that we simply accept trouble in a long-suffering way. But rather, it means that over the long haul we trust God and thereby have the unbreakable tenacity and stamina to carry on God's work without fear. Although many obstacles may be hurled in our path, "no weapon formed against us will prosper."

"No weapon that is formed against thee shall prosper; and every tongue that shall rise against thee in judgment thou shalt condemn. This is the heritage of the servants of the LORD, and their righteousness is of me, saith the LORD" (Is. 54:17, KJV).

Many people will challenge God's Word and His protection of His own, but will find that their efforts were a lost cause. To every challenge we may face, God's message to us is: "Everything is possible for him who believes" (Mark 9:23).

Fire is also a necessary component of lifelong victory. It is the ecstasy, the intoxication, the utter joy we experience as we become aware of the reality of God's love for us. With this fire comes the awakening of the Holy Spirit within us to want to love Him back, however poor our love for Him may be in comparison to His love for us. Passion for God becomes a magnificent obsession to rise above the dispassionate ordinary and to reach upward to catch hold of the extraordinary. Having this fire is to really be alive. In this fire is the desire to light the torch of the gospel and run with it to the ends of the earth, proclaiming the GOOD NEWS to all who will listen. When we have this fire, our hearts are so full of joy that it spills over and touches others, if only through the smiles with which we greet those we encounter.

Steadfastness is the third key component of running the race to the very end. With this, we never compromise in our beliefs. No matter how badly we are treated by other people or how difficult the hardships of life, we do not waiver in our allegiance to Christ.

All three of these attributes may be seen in the prophets of old and in those who have finished their good fight of faith in Christ.

> With courage in faith, we can all face death;
> Death receives but a fleeting nod,
> For our eyes will behold our victorious crown
> In the hands of the Son of God!

—— A Prayer ——

Dear God, I thank You for the availability of the power and faith that is necessary for me to courageously stay on the narrow path that leads to the gates of heaven which have been opened to me through Christ. Please equip me with the endurance, fire, and steadfastness that I need to fulfill Your will for my life. In Jesus Christ's name, I pray. Amen

⎯⎯ ≪ 11 ≫ ⎯⎯

THE CONDITION
OF FOLLOWING CHRIST

Then, speaking to all, [Jesus] said, "If anyone wants to
be a follower of mine, let him renounce himself and
take up his cross every day and follow me. Anyone who
wants to save his life will lose it; but anyone who loses
his life for my sake, will save it."

—LUKE 9:23–24, NEW JERUSALEM BIBLE

THE FATHER'S LOVE for us is so deep and encompass-
ing that He gave His own beloved Son as the innocent, spot-
less lamb to be sacrificed in our place so that our sins could
be washed away in His blood. Saying the words, "I believe in
Christ, who rose from the dead, and who is the Son of God,"
is a good start, but it's only a start. Mere words do not mean
much unless they are an expression of a heart that is devoted
to God—a heart that is filled with the spirit of Christ and
thereby beats along with the heart of Jesus.

There are those who appear to be devout followers of Christ
but proclaim that one has to be careful about making their

beliefs public. This seems to be particularly true for people in some sort of public limelight that are afraid they might lose respect if they let their beliefs be known. This is very dangerous ground on which to tread because Jesus warned against this very thing: "For if anyone is ashamed of me and of my words, of him the Son of man will be ashamed when he comes in his own glory and in the glory of the Father and the holy angels" (Luke 9:26, New Jerusalem Bible).

The loss of the spotlight seems quite trivial when one takes into account the fact that in many countries of the world many people are already risking, and in some cases giving up, their very lives when they gather in a home church, possess a page of scripture, tell someone they believe in Christ, or share the gospel with someone. This persecution will broaden to the western culture as well.

How trite is the fear of loss of position when compared to the honor those who come out of great tribulation will receive in heaven.

> These are they which came out of great tribulation, and have washed their robes, and made them white in the blood of the Lamb. Therefore are they before the throne of God, and serve him day and night in his temple: and he that sitteth on the throne shall dwell among them. They shall hunger no more, neither thirst any more; neither shall the sun light on them, nor any heat. For the Lamb which is in the midst of the throne shall feed them, and shall lead them unto living fountains of waters: and God shall wipe away all tears from their eyes.
>
> —REVELATION 7:14–17, KJV

Christians in western society have had it so easy and safe for so long that we have lost our fear, or awe, of God! Before long, however, our faith will be tested! Times will come that will require our faith to be rock-solid if we are not to faint in well doing. Someday we will look back on how trivial our concerns had once been and see how much we had really given ourselves to the vanity of this world. Now is the time to let God clean up the motives of our hearts so that we will be able to endure until we have finished our course here on earth.

The Father is merciful and just, abounding in love for those who love His Son and worship Him in Spirit and in truth. He also is waiting patiently for the return of His prodigal children. However, He will not wait forever. Jesus is coming soon to meet His true church in the air, leaving the lost behind.

Sifting out those parts of Scripture that warn that the way to heaven is straight and narrow is dangerous. The full counsel of God's Word is what contains God's redemptive plan for you and me.

> Every way of a man is right in his own eyes: but the LORD pondereth the hearts.
> —PROVERBS 21:2, KJV

> The way of a fool is right in his own eyes: but he that hearkeneth unto counsel is wise.
> —PROVERBS 12:15, KJV

God's love for mankind is so pure that I think He must be very perplexed as to why we are so stubborn that we do not always reach out to grasp His outstretched hand. Sometimes we think we are such clever little foxes, as we scamper down life's highway, doing things our own way—peeking out through the bushes to see if God is looking—when all the while He is standing right behind us, laughing and saying, "Got-cha!"

—— A PRAYER ——

Dear Father, all praise, honor, and glory be to You and Your beloved Son. Please give me the strength and endurance to follow in the footsteps of Christ, wherever they may lead. Please protect those people around the world who are laying their lives on the line in service to you. In Jesus Christ's name, I pray. Amen

────── ≪≫ 12 ≪≫ ──────

TO MEET THE LORD IN THE AIR

For the Lord Himself will come down from heaven,
with a loud command, with the voice of the archan-
gel and with the trumpet call of God, and the dead in
Christ will rise first. After that, we who are still alive
and are left will be caught up together with them in the
clouds to meet the Lord in the air.

—1 THESSALONIANS 4:16–17

THE SCRIPTURE ABOVE describes the Rapture. However, many people confuse this scripture with the Second
Coming of Christ.

After a number of casual conversations with people from
varying walks of life and Christian denominational persua-
sions, I have come to the realization that there is much confu-
sion about the time that is often referred to as the End Times.
Some believe there will be no Rapture. Others assume that
the Rapture is the Second Coming of Christ.

The Rapture, however, is not same event as the Second
Coming of Christ. At the time of the Second Coming, Jesus

Christ will actually come down upon the earth to put an end to the Great Tribulation and stop the horrendous slaughter at the battle of Armageddon, "lest there be no one left alive." Prior to this, Jesus will have met his church in the air already. Neither the Rapture nor the Second Coming of Christ means the end of the world, however. "That day will bring about the destruction of the heavens by fire, and the elements will melt in the heat. But in keeping with his promise we are looking forward to a new heaven and a new earth, the home of righteousness" (2 Pet. 3:12–13).

In Scripture, we read that people saw Jesus being taken up to heaven in a cloud. "He was taken up before their very eyes, and a cloud hid Him from their sight" (Acts 1:9). The Second Coming actually will be a time of violence. This important event is described in both the Old and New Testaments. One Old Testament prophecy of this is given in Isaiah:

> The hand of the Lord will be made known to his servants, but his fury will be shown to his foes. See, the Lord is coming with fire, and his chariots are like a whirlwind; he will bring down his anger and fury, and his rebuke with flames of fire. For with fire and with his sword the Lord will execute judgment upon all men, and many will be those slain by the Lord.
> —ISAIAH 66:14–16

Some people have a hard time reconciling the fact such a faithful and forgiving God, and such a loving and gentle Savior, also are full of the kind of justice described in the scriptures above. However, the character of God is multifaceted and the loving Savior soon will be returning as the Judge and King.

While most people cannot envision themselves doing

battle with the Lord and His church during the Battle of Armageddon, they do not realize that they are actually at war with Him when they do not repent of sin now. To repent of sin means that we turn away from the ways of the world and embrace the ways of God. One of those ways is forgiving others. This is so very important because forgiving others is a requirement for us to receive God's forgiveness. In order to forgive others, one exchanges attributes of self-centeredness for the selfless character of Christ.

Every person needs God's forgiveness. This is because all have sinned and come short of the glory of God (Rom. 3:23). Those who humbly ask for God's help and guidance can overcome their defects and boldly face the fact that their only hope is Jesus Christ. This is only possible when we stop blaming others for our faults, forgive those who have wronged us, and take the responsibility for partnering with the Lord to become more like Him every day. God's greatest blessings are always bestowed upon those who forgive.

We can lead others to Christ, but we can't save them! Only complete surrender to God will make that possible. Any sorrow that one might have now cannot come close to comparing with the suffering that lies in store for those who remain on earth during the Great Tribulation because they were not among those who met the Lord in the air.

If we embrace the Lord and his ways now, we will be greeted by the smiling face and outstretched arms of our beloved Savior, rather than by the fiery countenance of the conquering warrior of Armageddon—both of whom are Jesus Christ.

—— A Prayer ——

Dear Lord, I am in awe of You and of what You have prepared for Your faithful children. I trust in You and in Your ways. Please help me to embrace and rejoice over all of Your characteristics for You alone are God. In Jesus Christ's name, I pray. Amen.

⸺ ⚹ 13 ⚹ ⸺

ALL THAT MAN HAS
BELONGS TO GOD

To this John replied, "A man can receive only what is given to him from heaven... [Christ] must become greater; I must become less.

—JOHN 3:27, 30

AFTER JOHN THE Baptist had baptized Jesus, he testified, "'I myself did not know him, but the reason I came baptizing with water was that he might be revealed to Israel.'" Then John gave this testimony: "I saw the Spirit come down from heaven as a dove and remain on him. I would not have known him, except that the one who sent me to baptize with water told me, 'The man on whom you see the Spirit come down and remain is he who will baptize with the Holy Spirit'" (John 1:31–33).

Now, John's disciples were telling him that the man he had baptized and testified about was now baptizing people and everyone was now going to him instead of John. To this, John humbly answered that Jesus must become greater and he must become less. This wisdom must have come from above, for how else could John have known this? Although John's clothing was animal skins and his diet was locusts and honey, God had called him to the very special assignment of preparing the Jews for the ministry of Jesus. John lived, and then he died, fulfilling his destiny. In his life and in his death, he never denied the Messiah whom God revealed to him or tried to draw attention away from Jesus to himself.

John's testimony is one that all of us should heed when confronted with the temptation to puff ourselves up rather than redirecting all attention to the Lord. His testimony also serves as an exhortation for us to not be jealous when we see spiritual gifts at work in others. John's words indicate that he is celebrating the fact that God is now using Jesus instead of him to minister to the people, so much so that he said His joy was complete.

To this John replied, "A man can receive only what is given him from heaven. You yourselves can testify that I said, 'I am not the Christ but am sent ahead of him.' The bride belongs to the bridegroom. The friend who attends the bridegroom waits and listens for him, and is full of joy when he hears the bridegroom's voice. That joy is mine, and it is now complete." John 3:27–30.

Celebrating the fact that God is using other people is a way of praising God. God knew each of us long before we were even born. He, the Creator, has a plan for each one of us. He knows what each of us can and cannot handle. It could be that having a gift might cause us to stumble, and so, in his love, He has decided to gift us and use us in another way. Or it could be that more spiritual maturity is needed before the gift would not be a stumbling block or distraction to us.

> There are different kinds of gifts, but the same Spirit.
> There are different kinds of service, but the same Lord.
> There are different kinds of working, but the same God
> works all them in all men. All these are the work of one
> and the same spirit, and he gives them to each one, just
> as HE DETERMINES.
> —1 CORINTHIANS 12:4–6, 11, EMPHASIS ADDED

Although St. Paul mentions a number of spiritual gifts in 1 Corinthians, certainly not all of God's many gifts were listed there. He wrote a number of his epistles by candlelight in dark, dank prison cells. But, the light of his understanding of God's Word that was given to him would shine far beyond the flickering candle and would flood the world with God's love in the person of the Holy Spirit.

Through Christ's shed blood, we receive salvation. Both His death and His resurrection made the indwelling power of the Holy Spirit possible for us.

People often refer to a buildings as "the church." However, the church is much more than a building or a certain group of people who gather together for Christian fellowship and learning in one of those buildings. The church of the living God is the holy body of Christ with Christ as the head. The body of Christ is made up of many diverse parts, all working together to keep that precious body functioning well. However large or small the contribution may seem to be, each part is interdependent and part of the whole. We are all ONE in Christ!

To understand the functioning of the body of Christ, we can consider the marvelous functioning of the human body.

Each part has its own specific purpose. This is also true of the body of Christ: each part is important and the combination of the parts makes up the whole.

Envy, one of the seven deadly sins, as well as coveting, the tenth commandment, not only exists in secular society, but it rears its ugly head in the church. Using a bit of humor to expose and fight this defect helps take a bit of the sting out, and it also helps to open the eyes of the body of Christ. There are those among us who whine and complain when they see what God calls their neighbor to do. They pout and say, "He's nobody special! I've known him all my life!" And, "What about the lady in the upstairs apartment? God chooses her over me to do so much—I'm just as good as she is!" They begin to brood, thinking God must not love them very much because they feel they are nothing more important than the big toe on the foot of the body. If you are the big toe, rejoice! What if we didn't have big toes? We would be in a lot of trouble. It's our big toes that keep us balanced as we walk, especially if we are trying to walk in the footsteps of Christ.

If God's gift to you is that of a strong, unbreakable faith, be happy that He thought of you. If God calls you to give a cup of cold water to a tired, thirsty traveler, do it with love in your heart and a smile on your face. If God calls you to "knock down the walls of Jericho," then do it with the enthusiasm of a winner. Whether our actions are simple or stupendous—who cares? We are all ONE! The only one who can call himself the head of the body is Jesus Christ. He is the only One who can wear the crown as King of kings. When we realize the truth of this, we will begin to treat one another in a way that truly honors God and His wisdom.

When we come to the place where we are fitted jointly together in the Body of Christ, we will be functioning in a way that benefits the whole body of Christ and fulfills the purposes of God. Our joy then will be full, like John the Baptist's was, when we realize that we are preparing the way for the Second Coming of Christ.

—— A PRAYER ——

Dear God, all praise, honor, and glory be to You and Your beloved Son. We thank You for all the varied spiritual gifts you have bestowed upon us. Please help us to guard ourselves against becoming so filled with spiritual avarice to do good, that we miss the target of doing Your will. God, have mercy on us and guide us to use each of our gifts to their fullest potential. We love You. We worship You. In Jesus' name we pray. Amen

——— ⫷ 14 ⫸ ———

DO NOT LOVE THE WORLD

Do not love the world or anything in the world. If anyone loves the world, the love of the Father is not in him. For everything in the world—the cravings of sinful man, the lust of his eyes and the boasting of what he has and does—comes not from the Father but from the world. The world and its desires pass away, but the man who does the will of God lives forever.

—1 JOHN 2:15–17

T O THE PEOPLE whose lives are lived for and surrendered to their Father in heaven, the scriptures noted above bring peace and comfort. This is not the case, however, for people who try to live halfway between the ways of the world and the love of the Father. There really is no halfway point, however. A person is either saved or lost. Even after we have become a part of the body of Christ, however, we will be bombarded with doctrines that water down the truth of God's Word. This is actually one of the ways Satan uses in his effort to lull us back into the trap of sin.

These bombardments may even come from behind the

pulpits of churches. Being girded with the armor of God and remembering that Jesus is the same, yesterday, today, and forever, is a way to avoid being lulled by inaccurate opinions of what God's Word says and who He is.

God's Word is the same yesterday, today, and forever! No one on this earth is immune from either the covering or the conviction of His word. Mankind hasn't changed much since the Garden of Eden. All praise, honor, and glory belong to both Father and Son, and if we truly repent (meaning we are willing to allow God to change us, and to grow in the light of His Holy Spirit), His blessings upon us will become undreamed-of miracles. How could we not believe this when we think of the tortured, broken, bleeding body of our Savior, hanging helplessly on the cross? Close your eyes for a moment and look upon His agony. Now, do you comprehend the magnitude of what Christ did for all humanity? He didn't just die—He conquered death and sin and rose again so that we might also have the chance to do the same!

We cannot afford to become like a pendulum on a grandfather clock, swinging to and fro between God's truth and the sweet sounding, compelling lies of the world. Nothing of the world's accusing imaginations comes from God. These clever manipulators exist in secular society and in the church, like "tares among the wheat." Gird yourself with the armor of Christ, and block the pathway of Satan!

We must come to terms with the fact that we are living in the "end times." Those who truly know and belong to God have the peace that passes all understanding and find this to be a thrilling time to be alive. Those who are not sure where they stand, spiritually, may think this is a time of insecurity and terror, however. Suddenly their comfort zone has been shaken. They can no longer pretend to themselves and others that they are on their way to heaven even though their hearts and lives are not His. They can no longer act like they are eternally safe, for the love of the Father is not in them.

Saying words that profess belief are not sufficient. We must do God's will if we are to spend eternity with Him and have spiritual riches to touch the lives and hearts of others during our time here on earth. God gives to us in generous portions, and one aspect of His will is for us to reach out into the community and the world generously. He wants us to reach and rescue the lost lambs who are searching for Him, even if they do not realize that they are. It is for us to warn people that they must fulfill God's will and not rest in the fact that they prayed a prayer long ago that spoke of belief in God. This is the magnificent obsession of God's love for all mankind. It is always spreading outward into the world like a pebble tossed into a pond, and the ripples it causes never seem to end! The world, with all its hollow attractions and false promises will soon fade into oblivion as our eyes behold the wonders of everything that God has in store for those who do His will.

—— A PRAYER ——

Dear God, thank You for giving me all I need to fulfill Your will for my life. Please give me Your love for the lost and the boldness I need to warn people that they must do Your will. In Jesus Christ's name, I pray. Amen.

—— ⪻ 15 ⪼ ——

PARABLES:
SECRETS OF THE KINGDOM

The disciples came to him and asked, "Why do you speak to the people in parables?" He replied, "The knowledge of the secrets of the kingdom of heaven has been given to you, but not to them. Whoever has will be given more, and he will have an abundance. Whoever does not have, even what he has will be taken from him. This is why I speak in parables: 'Though seeing, they do not see; though hearing, they do not hear or understand. In them is fulfilled the prophecy of Isaiah: 'You will be ever hearing, but never understanding; you will be ever seeing but never perceiving. For this people's heart has become calloused; they hardly hear with their ears, and they have closed their eyes. Otherwise they might see with their eyes, hear with their ears, understand with their hearts and turn, and I would heal them.'"

—MATTHEW 13:10–15

THE ABOVE SCRIPTURES bring me sadness today when I think of them in the context of the fact that so many people's hearts are calloused still. From Jesus' time until now, people have perceived God's Word through an earth-bound view rather than through a spiritual one. Because they have not turned to the Savior so that He might heal them and make them alive in Him, they remain blind, deaf, and dumb to the things of the Spirit.

Those people who have received Christ and speak God's Word without compromise are fulfilling God's will on earth. These messengers understand the eternal significance of standing firm in His Word in spite of the opposition.

When God lights a candle to shatter the darkness in human lives, it exposes all the blemishes behind the façades. The Spirit of God is what opens eyes to truth and exposes the darkness. The Spirit of God is what gives the messengers the boldness to speak the truth in love. When we go into battle for souls, we must be like Daniel: his strength and safety came from his relentless allegiance to God. He lived to please God—not other people.

> Do not be deceived: God cannot be mocked. A man reaps what he sows. The one who sows to please his sinful nature, from that nature will reap destruction; the one who sows to please the Spirit, from the Spirit will reap eternal life.
>
> —GALATIANS 6:7–8

Indwelling faith without works is disobeying God. But works without indwelling faith is worth nothing at all.

> Surely the Sovereign Lord does nothing without revealing his plan to his servants the prophets.
>
> —AMOS 3: 7

God's revelations through the prophets are not meant to condemn or judge mankind, but are meant to warn and awaken them if they are going in the wrong direction. God never gives a warning without giving a solution. If you have eyes—then see! If you have ears—then hear! If you have a heart—then understand! The Spirit of God is ever hovering over us, waiting to find a home in our hearts. He wants to reveal His plans to His people for the sake of His people and for the sake of those who are still to be drawn to Him.

—— A PRAYER ——

Dear God, all praise, honor, and glory be to You and Your beloved Son. We pray that the eyes, ears, and hearts of people be opened so that we may comprehend the awesome power of Your love. Guide us to the knowledge of the secrets of Your kingdom. Many have strayed from Your golden pathway, yet You patiently wait for their return. We pray in Jesus' name; guide the lost wanderers home. Amen.

——— 《 16 》 ———

BLESSED ARE THOSE
WHO TRUST IN THE LORD

How lovely is your dwelling place, O LORD Almighty!
My soul yearns, even faints, for the courts of the Lord;
my heart and my flesh cry out for the living God. Blessed
are those whose strength is in you. They go from strength
to strength, till each appears before God in Zion. Better
is one day in your courts than a thousand elsewhere; I
would rather be a doorkeeper in the house of my God
than dwell in the tents of the wicked. For the Lord God
is a sun and shield; the Lord bestows favor and honor;
no good thing does he withhold from those whose walk
is blameless. O LORD Almighty, blessed is the man who
trusts in you.

—PSALM 84:1, 2, 5, 7, 10–12

M AY I BE so bold as to paint a word picture of what
God is seeing as He sits upon His throne above and looks
down upon the earth and its myriad of inhabitants? God sees
many a church that is a beautiful citadel, aloof and unfeel-
ing, standing on immaculate green lawns and beds of lovely
flowers. A church, oblivious to the noisy bustle of traffic, and
totally blind and deaf to the yearnings of earth's masses moving before Him like the restless undulations of the oceans.
This is but a stone building, and the true church is the living,
blood-soaked body of Christ sheltered by these structures we
so proudly maintain.

Not all who sit within the protective covering of a church building have found Christ. Not all scholars, spending a lifetime searching and dissecting scripture, have found Him. Indeed, not even all the ecumenical hierarchy have found Him. There is a vast difference between knowing *about* Christ and *actually knowing* Him. Until Christ lives in our hearts, we cannot comprehend the fullness of God's Word.

Words betray the heart! That which is hidden in the human heart ultimately comes out of the mouth, both God's truth and the devil's lies. Until we have learned to let God change us, until we have learned to listen and obey God's Word, instead of always being the one talking, nothing we say edifies the true church. The hearts filled with the Holy Spirit also have mouths filled with praise and thanksgiving given to God, and their words guide others to kneel down before His throne in worship and adoration, which last into eternity.

Earth is just one relatively small planet in the vast universe created by God. Yet, it is His pet project. We can assume this to be true because this is where He sent His own beloved Son, Jesus Christ, to redeem its inhabitants. This is also where the Comforter, the Holy Spirit has come, and where He has placed His church, the living body of Christ.

Knowing that the fulfillment of His plan on earth is so important to Him can be a great comfort to us when we realize that we are a part of something so very special. After we become a part of the body of Christ, we are at the beckoning of the mind of the body—Jesus Christ. He is the brain and we the parts that do the brain's bidding. This is why it is so very important to keep our minds and hearts pure. Only then can we receive and respond to directions from the Lord. Only then will we trust the Lord enough to obey His will rather than do what we might be naturally inclined to do.

——— **A PRAYER** ———

Dear God, fill our hearts and souls with a burning desire to worship You in Your courts; to fall down before You in reverence at the foot of Your throne, and to hear You say, "Rise up! Well done my good and faithful servant." We pray in Jesus' name for the whole, dying war-torn world, and for her helpless, starving, desperate inhabitants. We are sorry, Lord, that our disobedience toward Your Word and will has made such a mess out of a world that you so lovingly created for us. Amen.

——— ≪ 17 ≫ ———

AND THE WALLS
CAME 'TUMBLIN DOWN

They say to seers, "See no more visions!" and to the
prophets, "Give us no more visions of what is right! Tell
us pleasant things, prophesy illusions. Leave this way,
get off this path and stop confronting us with the Holy
One of Israel!" Therefore this is what the Holy One of
Israel says: "Because you have rejected this message,
relied on oppression and depended on deceit, this sin
will become for you like a high wall, cracked and bulg-
ing. that collapses suddenly in an instant."

—ISAIAH 30:10–13

When you spread out your hands in prayer, I will hide
my eyes from you; even if you offer many prayers, I will
not listen.

—ISAIAH 1:15

I T SEEMS THAT prophecy is coming true everywhere we
turn. Isaiah, one of the greatest prophets of all time, probably
had no concept that the messages sent to him by God were
not just for the Hebrew people, but also would apply to people belonging to nations that did not even exist in his time.

One kind of apostasy that is taking place now, thousands
of years after Isaiah's time, is various church denominations'
acceptance of homosexuality even though it is referred to as an
abomination in many areas of the Bible, including Leviticus
18:22. Barring birth defects, this is an acquired choice—not

something a person is born with. Orientation is a modern-day word of excuse for the church to accept this life choice. But the watered down labeling does not change the fact that it still remains an abomination to the Lord.

The fact that one denomination actually promoted an active homosexual to the position of bishop almost dumbfounds anyone who has even casually read the Bible. How can someone who actively practicing this abomination possibly be considered a moral or spiritual leader to anyone? This man claims God called him to this position so that he could draw these people into the safety and saving grace of the church. God's true church, however, teaches exactly the opposite of what he represents. God will accept the homosexuals if they truly repent and change direction. God will never turn His back on anyone who sincerely wants to recover! But, He certainly won't cater to people who live this way even if the example of a false prophet tells them that it is okay for them to continue on in that sin. This apostasy is just one example of how we must beware of teachers of false doctrine and those who live contrary to the Word of God. It also illustrates that people can speak from the unction of an unholy spirit and claim it to be from the Holy Spirit.

Scripture teaches the good moral values just as it teaches the good spiritual values. God gives us these guidelines for our own safety, both physical and spiritual. Those people who misinterpret or misrepresent the Bible are in grave danger of a fire that will eternally consume them and anyone who follows their teachings.

> For if someone comes to you and preaches a Jesus other than the Jesus we preached, or if you receive a different spirit from the one you received, or a different gospel from the one you accepted, you put up with easily

enough. For such men are false apostles, deceitful work-men, masquerading as apostles of Christ. And no won-der, for Satan himself masquerades as an angel of light. It is not surprising, then, if his servants masquerade as servants of righteousness. Their end will be what their actions deserve.

—2 CORINTHIANS 11:4, 13–15

Homosexuals should not be abused or shunned by the church or society. They should be treated with care and patience. Receiving solid Biblical teachings may be the only chance they have of turning their lives around. However, until such time as they have changed, no leadership positions of any kind in the church should be awarded to them. Also, no same-sex marriages should ever be sanctified by the church, lest we become another Sodom and Gomorrah.

The Bible must be our guiding post. By knowing and understanding it well, we will be able to discern the false prophets. It is important that we not be afraid of being accused of judging. In my years of experience, the only ones who piously say, "I don't judge," are the ones who do not want to hear God's truth.

Another form of apostasy today is found in caricatures of Jesus in the media, and even in the church, that deny the deity of Christ and majesty of the Father. Another attack against the church also comes from secular society and within the church. It is the attack on the plan of salvation. I've actually heard a televangelist say, "You are already forgiven by God! You don't even have to tell God you are sorry for all your sins!" The words of the false prophet went out over the airways in TV land and many words like that are being heard in other forms of media and even from behind church pulpits. Christ fervently warned of strong consequences of causing one of his children to sin: "But if anyone causes one of these little ones who believe in me to sin, it would be better for him to have a large millstone hung around his neck and to be drowned in the depths of the sea. Woe to the world because of the things that cause people to sin! Such things must come, but woe to the man through whom they come!" (Matt. 18:6–7).

Those of us who know the truth of God's Word must be bold in the faith when faced with the opportunity to expose the false teaching of false prophets who would cause people to stay in sin or return to it. Our motivation must be in love, in knowing that it is the Lord's compassion that sounds the alarm.

"Yet the Lord longs to be gracious to you; he rises to show you compassion, For the Lord is a God of justice. Blessed are all who wait for him!" (Isa. 30:18)

―――― **A Prayer** ――――

Dear God, all praise and honor belongs to You. Please emblazon in our hearts and souls the power and strength of Your Holy Word, so that no false prophet can convince us of any false teaching. Help us to expose lies by walking in and speaking truth. In Jesus Christ's name, I pray. Amen.

18

PUT ON THE FULL ARMOR
OF CHRIST

Finally, grow strong in the Lord, with the strength of his power. Put on the full armour of God so as to be able to resist the devil's tactics.
—Ephesians 6:10–11, New Jerusalem Bible

And he said to them, "The harvest is rich, but the labourers are few, so ask the Lord of the harvest to send labourers to do his harvesting."
—Luke 10:2, New Jerusalem Bible

THE BEGINNERS IN faith, like little children and the newly converted, are fed spiritual milk by being told "Jesus loves them"; the Bible says so. This is the best of beginnings and teachings. But we cannot spend the rest of our lives like baby ducks, paddling around in puddles of milk! God expects us to grow into the full stature of Christ with the meat of His Holy Word and Spirit.

Each church congregation in the world is the spiritual manifestation of the body of Christ on earth. We are commissioned by God to keep His precious Son's body strong and healthy. How dare we, then, do things that batter and bruise our Lord? Why the stubbed toes in the body that, hypothetically, come from kicking others? Why the sore throat that comes from the battery-acid words that never should have been spoken? Why the itching that comes from a rash caused by petty, nit-picking criticism against the efforts of others, including against the shepherd that God sends to feed His flock with spiritual truth? Why the migraine headaches that come from those who constantly hit their heads against the wall because they don't always get their own way? Again, I say, *How dare we cripple Christ's body like this?* When our human bodies are hurting, we have a greatly diminished capacity to function as individuals, let alone the incapacity of the body of Christ, who is meant to accomplish God's will on earth!

Each of us must vow to attend diligently to the health of our Lord's body. We do this by loving one another, caring for the needs of others, and defending and aiding the less fortunate. We must encourage everyone's endeavor to do God's will, and teach and protect our children because they are our future. We must pay attention to our elderly, letting them know that they are still a vital part of Christ's body. Then, God Himself will cover us with the strong and shining armor of Jesus. When this happens, look out world. For, then, God's miracles will begin to appear in abundance among us.

Too often we become so self-absorbed in carving out our own little corner of salvation that we cannot hear the groaning of the souls outside our walls, whom God says we must reap for His harvest. Unfortunately, there are those who think that by paying their "dues" (what some call their offerings), by donating generously to mission projects, by faithfully attending church, and by saying all the expected holy words, they have done all the necessary "Christian" participation. That kind of mind-set is about as effective for God as a flat tire! There is a sad fact, however, that we must realize: not everyone, by their own volition, can be reached! No matter how sincere we may be in our efforts to lead them to Christ, sometimes our efforts will fall on deaf ears. While this is true, it does not change the fact that it would be a crime if the laborers were so few that perfectly beautiful fruit would be left to rot on the vine, and wheat fields would dry up and blow away in the wind. I believe God will hold all Christendom accountable for this tragic waste.

We are at the brink of eternity today, where Christ stands tall, strong, and healthy. He is poised and waiting to return to earth to claim His harvest. Here, at the brink of eternity, it is time for the body of Christ also to be standing tall, strong, and healthy in expectation and preparation of Christ's return.

——— A PRAYER ———

Dear God, instill in our hearts the ability to care for others enough to lead them to Christ. We must feed them, clothe and comfort them. But help us to understand that loving our neighbors as ourselves and loving our enemies really means that we want salvation for them as much as we want it for ourselves. By the power of the Holy Spirit, help us to grow big enough to wear the armor of Christ, in whose name we pray! Amen.

─── ≪ 19 ≫ ───

THE BIBLE—
THE GREATEST STORIES EVER TOLD

T HE BIBLE IS filled with some of the most powerful and dynamic literature ever written. The stories are true, not fiction. The lessons and morals contained there are truth, wisdom, and redemption. Here, I will present a synopsis of one of the greatest.

Samuel, a chosen prophet of God, was commissioned by God to fulfill the people's clamorous request for a king. The Lord led Samuel to Saul, the son of Kish. He was a strong, handsome man standing a head taller than others. The people shouted, "Long live the King!" Saul was approximately thirty years old when be became Israel's first earthly king, and he reigned over Israel forty years. Samuel anointed him, and God changed Saul's heart when the spirit of God came upon him. Saul was a warrior king, and much of his reign was carried out in battle.

One day God commanded Saul to attack the Amalekites. He was told to obliterate totally every man, woman, child, and infant. He was also to kill all their animals. This order was given because the Amalekites had so badly abused the Israelites when they had come up from Egypt. Saul attacked and was victorious, but he took their King Agag as hostage and only destroyed the weak animals. In failing to kill the king and the best of the sheep, cattle, and fatted calves, Saul disobeyed God and did things his own way.

Then, the word of God came to Samuel and told him that He was grieved that Saul disobeyed his instructions. Samuel was very troubled and cried all night to God, asking Him to spare Saul's kingship. But, God's anger could not be allayed, and He said He would choose another king. When Samuel confronted Saul, Saul lied and claimed he had accomplished all God had asked, all except for one tiny thing. He had spared the life of Agag and saved the best of the animals for burnt offerings to God. To this, Samuel replied, "Does the Lord delight in burnt offerings and sacrifices as much as in obeying the voice of the Lord?" (1 Sam. 15:22). In other words, Samuel was saying that God is much more concerned about our obedience than our gifts!

Saul tried to blame others for his sin, "I have sinned. I violated the Lord's command and your instructions. I was afraid of the people, and so I gave in to them" (1 Sam. 15:24). Samuel then asked that Agag be brought to him, and Samuel put Agag to death in the presence of Saul and the others (verse 33). Saul begged Samuel not to leave him, but the prophet walked away and never saw Saul again (verses 34, 35).

God was grieved that He had ever made Saul a king over Israel, and He sent Samuel to Jesse of Bethlehem. There, David was set apart to be a future king. Samuel anointed David with oil, and from that day on, the Spirit of the Lord came upon David in power. The Spirit of the Lord had departed from Saul, and an evil spirit tormented him.

Saul loved the music of the harp—it soothed his disturbed, tormented soul. He had heard of the talent of this shepherd boy named David and sent servants to ask for David's father, Jesse, to send David to minister to him. Saul was pleased with David and requested that he remain in his service as an armor-bearer. David and Saul's son, Jonathan, became the best of friends—a friendship that even Saul's treachery would not break.

Little by little, David became well-known to the people. His fearless encounter with Goliath was the beginning of his notoriety. Then when he was successful in battle, the people began shouting, "Saul has slain his thousands, and David his ten of thousands" (1 Sam. 18:7). Resentment began to well up in Saul's heart, and he became very jealous of David. An evil spirit came upon him. From that time on, Saul kept a hateful, jealous eye on David.

Once, David had been called to play for Saul. Saul suddenly became enraged and hurled a spear at David, hoping to pin David to the wall, but David eluded him twice. Several more times Saul's hatred drove him to seek help from others in his determination to kill David. Warned of Saul's intentions, David fled. Both Saul and Jonathan died in battle. Jonathan died by the spear of the enemy, and Saul, in his grief over his son's death, by his own sword. In spite of Saul's treachery, David had never raised his hand against the king. David mourned for both of them. Eventually, David became the king of Judah—but that's another story.

This scenario sounds a lot like a Shakespearean tragedy, but it is a true story right out of the pages of Old Testament history, 1 Sam. 15–31. Its message of severe consequences for disobeying God's word and direction is as relevant today as it was then. Today, however, we live in a dispensation of grace in which we have access to forgiveness and redemption through Jesus. It is not God, Christ, or others who condemn or judge anyone.

> For prophecy never had its origin in the will of man, but men spoke from God as they were carried along by the Holy Spirit.
> —2 PETER 1: 21

That scripture not only applies to prophets of old, but also to today's prophets. None of my writings come out of my own imagination. Saul and the Pharisees of Christ's time on earth had much in common when it came to arrogant feelings of self-importance and self-sufficiency. Christ had some pretty harsh words for the Pharisees, and yet, his love for all mankind was such that He died for them too.

In meditating on the story of Saul's loss of his position as king, we can see a warning for us to be very careful to not rely on our own abilities and thereby short-circuit what God has for us to do.

—— A PRAYER ——

Our Father who art in heaven, hallowed be Thy name. Thy kingdom come, Thy will be done on earth as it is in heaven. Give us this day our daily bread, and forgive us our sins as we forgive those who sin against us. Lead us not into temptation, but deliver us from evil. For Thine is the kingdom, and the power, and the glory forever and ever more. Amen.

—※ 20 ※—

THE HEART OF MARY REVEALED—
THE MAGNIFICAT

And Mary said: "My soul glorifies the Lord and my
spirit rejoices in God my Savior, for he has been mind-
ful of the humble state of his servant. From now on all
generations will call me blessed, for the Mighty One
has done great things for me—holy is his name. His
mercy extends to those who fear him, from generation
to generation. He has performed mighty deeds with
his arm; he has scattered those who are proud in their
inmost thoughts. He has brought down rulers from
their thrones but has lifted up the humble. He has
filled the hungry with good things but has sent the rich
away empty."

—LUKE 1:46–53

MARY, YOUNG AS she was, never doubted her God!
In whatever we do—in whatever we accomplish, let it be only
to glorify God and edify his holy church! Few people perceive the unseen spiritual level that ever hovers over us. Most
people fail to grasp this magnificent reality and strive only
for the "rewards" in this life. Instead, they view believers who
live at this level as a threat to the images they have crafted of
themselves. As a sad result, they spend a lifetime wallowing
around in the mud of mediocrity, never "seeing or perceiving"
that there is so much more to what God calls us to become in
the light of his Holy Spirit!

Little Mary's song—the Magnificat—revealed spiritual wisdom far beyond her tender years when she said, "He has used the power of His arm. He has scattered the proud of heart. He has pulled down rulers from their thrones and lifted up the humble." Mary portrays the loving, trusting, obedient heart of a chosen child of God. She was totally submissive to fulfilling the will of God even though it meant facing the disgrace and derision of her village and her family, and the risk of losing the love and respect of the man she would never stop loving for as long as she lived—Joseph. She could have even been stoned to death. But, her faith in God's ability to clear the path for His will to be accomplished never wavered.

Throughout all history, whether on the secular or spiritual level, God allows the "arrogant of heart" to function and influence vital decisions for just so long, until He decides that enough is enough! Especially in the end times in which we are living, the power of His mighty arm has, and will, rout the haughty, pull down the rulers from their thrones, and raise high the lowly. The Pharisees of Christ's era, who tried to religiously dictate that everything be done their way, were defeated by Christ's life, teachings, death, and resurrection. Christ is now lifting up the "lowly" in the church, and His mighty arm is protecting them so that they may blossom and flourish without fear of criticism from modern-day Pharisees.

Just as God has the power to bring down the haughty, He also has the power to lift them back up and forgive all sins against Him if they humbly approach Him with a repentant heart and pray for forgiveness. He welcomes his prodigal children with open arms. We are all different from each other, and what we are like determines how God is forced to deal with us. At the time of Jesus' baptism, the Holy Spirit, like a dove, quietly descended from heaven and settled upon Jesus. This was indicative of the fact that Jesus' heart was open, loving, gentle, and obedient to the will of God.

Saul of Tarsus, on the other hand, was an arrogant, stubborn, hardheaded Pharisee who was from the tribe of Benjamin and took great pleasure in arresting and persecuting Christians, ultimately being responsible for their deaths. God, literally, had to knock this murderer off his horse, lay him flat on his back, and blind him for three days to get his attention.

These two illustrations show how the Father deals with different people in different ways. With this in mind, we must never doubt God's love for us, regardless of what manner He deals with us.

If we cannot accept His gentle chastening, He will be forced to deal with us more harshly. Unless a seed is planted in the ground, and dies unto itself, it will never reach the destiny for which it was created. In His love, God will deal with us harshly to get our attention.

The minute we take our eyes off of Jesus, we are in spiritual and physical danger. Even Peter was able to walk on water until, in one nanosecond, he took his eyes off of Jesus and became so self-centered in fear that "whoosh" he went down and under, screaming for the Master to save him. The strong arm of Jesus lifted him back into the boat, and Jesus said, "You of little faith, why did you doubt?" (Matt. 14:31). There was a man who doubted his God even though He was standing right in front of him. Even when we are being chastened by the Lord, we must keep our focus fixed on Him rather than on the circumstance we are in at the time.

—— A PRAYER ——

Dear God, by the power and might of Your arm, lift me and Your people up in these final days, to accomplish the destiny You have ordained for each believer. Please give us the faith, strength, and courage to do Your will. With all my heart, I give You my life—let it ever be to serve You! In Jesus Christ's name, I pray. Amen.

—— ≪ 21 ≫ ——

THE ENIGMA

Do not think that I have come to abolish the Law or
the Prophets; I have not come to abolish them, but to
fulfill them. I tell you the truth, until heaven and earth
disappear, not the smallest letter, not the least stroke of
a pen, will by any means disappear from the Law until
everything is accomplished. Anyone who breaks one of
the least of these commandments and teaches others
to do the same will be called least in the kingdom of
heaven, but whoever practices and teaches these com-
mands will be called great in the kingdom of heaven.
For I tell you that unless your righteousness surpasses
that of the Pharisees and the teachers of the law, you will
certainly not enter the kingdom of heaven.

—MATTHEW 5:17–20

J ESUS SAID THAT He did not come to abolish or replace
the Law of Moses. Instead, He came to fulfill it. When talking to the Pharisees, He rebuked them for piling burdens on
the backs of the people that they could not possibly carry.
The Pharisees' dictates were not even contained in the Law
of Moses. He also noted that the Pharisees themselves were
not even fulfilling the religious requirements that they were
imposing on the people.

Jesus spoke new words of God's wisdom that the people
had never heard before. For the first time, the poor suffering masses began to see a ray of hope and anticipation. Jesus'

words shed light on the tyranny of unjust authority rooted in religious hypocrisy.

As the words given Him by His Father began to take root in the consciousness of the people and be confirmed with miracles, fear sprung up in the hearts of the Pharisees, and they brought false accusations against Him. They raged loudly at Him even though his answers always confounded them. The accusations against Jesus and His teachings still rage on today, more than two thousand years after His death and resurrection: "A fool finds no pleasure in understanding, but delights in airing his own opinions" (Prov. 18:2). Even so, however, God never changes and always has the solution for any problem. Also, God still sends answers through those who, like Jesus, are tuned in to hear His still, small voice and obey it.

It is often the Spirit-filled pastors who awaken a lasting presence of Christ in the hearts of their parishioners. It is the shepherd who preaches the fullness of God's Word—not a watered down interpretation of it—that brings his flock to unbreakable faith in the Lord and leads them to the glory of eternal life. The unpretentious man of God who delivers the power of God's Word is the one who guides people into the fold and directs them into the harvest field.

God also uses the members of the flock to minister to one another and to others. By Christ's stripes we are healed. The gentle touch of a hand, a kiss on the cheek or forehead, and faith-filled prayers are all ways through which the miracle of healing flows: "By whose stripes you were healed" (1 Pet. 2:24, NKJV). God, and only God, does the healing, and all the thanksgiving and glory belong to Him. For some instances of healing, God sends the specific words that are needed to reach the heart of the afflicted person and to strengthen their faith in believing that God's blessings have been given to them. The same healing words, given to one person, may not be the same words that would reach and heal another. All healing comes from God, and He knows what each person needs to hear. The words that God gives to His faithful servants through His still, small voice ignite faith and bring healing to those for whom prayers are being prayed.

Complete healing is seldom instantaneous. Instead, it is often a process that may take weeks or months to complete. The key is to keep your eyes fixed on Jesus and believe you are healed. Even though you may have a time when things look pretty bleak, keep the fire of faith burning.

> Christ was as strong as a lion – yet, weak as a lamb.
> He was sure of His identity – yet, humble as a servant.
> He was sorely tempted and abused – yet, a forgiving God.
> He was a man of sorrow – yet, His words brought songs of joy.
> He was wise as the serpents – yet, gentle as a dove.
> He was patient as virtue itself – yet, in righteous wrath drove the money scalpers off the temple steps.
>
> He is God's undefeatable warrior – yet, is peace that passeth all understanding.
> He is wise as wisdom itself – yet, praised the innocent trust of a child
> He was a miracle worker – yet, gave credit and glory only to God.
> He sweated fearful drops of blood at Gethsemane – yet said, "Thy will be done."
> He died a sinner – yet, was pure as fired gold.
> He died forsaken by most of His followers – yet, lives forevermore.
> It is given to mankind once to die – yet, because of Him, we will also rise to eternal life.

Christ is the ultimate ENIGMA – yet, the ANSWER
to every riddle life can throw at us!

—— **A PRAYER** ——

*Dear God, all praise, honor, glory and allegiance belong to
You. Thank You, Jesus, that by Your stripes we are healed.
Please give me the ears to hear Your still, small voice so that
I can be used to ignite faith for healing in others. Show
Your people Your miraculous power so that Your love will
be manifested in a way that causes the lost to know that You
are all-powerful. In Jesus Christ's name, I pray. Amen.*

── ❧ 22 ❧ ──

WARNING TO PAY ATTENTION

We must pay more careful attention, therefore, to what we have heard, so that we do not drift away. For if the message spoken by angels was binding, and every violation and disobedience received its just punishment, how shall we escape if we ignore such a great salvation? This salvation, which was first announced by the Lord, was confirmed to us by those who heard him. God also testified to it by signs, wonders and various miracles, and gifts of the Holy Spirit distributed according to his will.

—HEBREWS 2:1–4

ALL PRAISE, HONOR, allegiance, love, and worship be given to our Father and Savior! It belongs to them, with every breath we breathe, with every beat of our hearts, and with every song of joy our souls can sing! Because of Christ's sacrifice and resurrection, we now have the Holy Spirit here with us.

His sacrifice, however, must be highly valued. For, like Esau, if we are not vigilant, we can sell our inheritance for a "mess of pottage." We assume God's love for us is so great that we can waste much of our lives entertaining ourselves with meaningless, selfish activities. This may happen when we think our salvation is assured just because Jesus died and rose again for us. This perspective may seem sugary sweet but the whole Word of God also includes the bitter aftertaste of lifelong repentance from sin and service to self. In Revelation 10:9–11 and Ezekiel 3:3, we read of how God's words may taste so sweet in the mouth, but once swallowed, turn sour in the stomach. While it is true that our redemption is very sweet, we must not take it for granted if we are to finish our course without selling out.

The true church, the body of Christ, is awakening like the great sleeping giant that it really always has been. Eyes, ears, and hearts are being brought to life with graphic understanding of why we are alive—and most of all, what God wants from us. First of all, He wants us to worship Him, and only Him, which is the first of the Ten Commandments. We are also called to do good for others; to lead as many as possible to Christ. Doing "good works" is required of true Spirit-filled believers, but it is not the impetus of our being. We must be careful that we are not doing the right thing, the wrong way, or for the wrong reason.

Christ came to give us life filled with abundance. That abundance, however, is not what we are to seek. Instead, we are to seek first the kingdom of God and his righteousness: "But seek ye first the kingdom of God, and his righteousness; and all these things shall be added unto you" (Matt. 6:33).

The church that is awakening is being filled so full of God's blessings that I can feel its overflowing spirit moving into the world with relevance! Now the fun and fellowship among God's people is counting for something that will touch and move the mountains of apathy that have been holding the true church back. I will never stop being amazed at the wondrous way God works. His love encompasses the whole earth and each tiny segment of His creation. Often, we do not discern God's intentions through His actions and messages, but when our focus remains intent on him, He sometimes reveals what is on His heart.

In Joel 2:28 we read that in the latter days God will pour out His spirit upon all flesh. A dynamic revival of passion for God and His beloved Son is coming. A revival is needed because this passion has been smothered and stifled for many years by watered-down preaching from pastors who have been afraid that the people would not tolerate the fullness of God's truth. My message to shepherds all over the world is this: You don't have to be afraid of the Pharisees—the tares among the wheat who may be among your congregations; God is ever present and watching over you. He will stop the arrogant hypocrites from harming your ministry. If you are telling God's truth in its total fullness, remember this, "No weapon that is formed against you will prosper" (Isaiah 54:17, New Jerusalem Bible).

Above all, we must love and worship both Father and Son! The proof of our love for God comes to life when we invite another to come and walk the highway to heaven with us. This cannot be relegated to pastors, priests, and prophets. Every part of the body of Christ must be a part of this Great Commission. For, there is great rejoicing in heaven when just one lost lamb has been reached and rescued!

—— **A PRAYER** ——

Dear God, may thy kingdom come, may thy will be done, on earth as it is in heaven! In Jesus Christ's name, I pray. Amen

—— ⫷ 23 ⫸ ——

TIMING IS EVERYTHING

Whoever obeys his command will come to no harm, and the wise heart will know the proper time and procedure. For there is a proper time and procedure for every matter.

—ECCLESIASTES 8:5–6

HOW MANY TIMES have we all heard the cliché, "Timing is everything"? As each day of my life has passed, I have become aware that this is not just a cliché, but a golden portal of wisdom. It also is a door that I have banged my head against more than once.

However good our intentions, we all have the tendency to either "rush" everything or procrastinate. Rushing God's timetable is a sign of immaturity. When we do this, we do not give God time to set the scene, as it were, so that His goodness will come in fullness. Waiting too long to act may result in missing the opportunity altogether. How embarrassing, or sometimes tragic, to be left standing on the dock, watching our ship of opportunity sail into the sunset!

God's timing is everything. Christ was born at just the right time. He led a quiet, common, ordinary life for thirty years. Then, just at the right time, He burst forth upon the scene with His wisdom from God, backed up by His miracles. Just at God's predestined time, Jesus was led to the cross. Just at the right time, God's Lamb rose from the dead to certify eternal life for Himself and for all who humbly follow Him, with His Spirit living within them. Just at the right time, He ascended into heaven in the presence of His disciples and many other witnesses. Just at the right time, He will return in the clouds to call His bride up to Him in the Rapture. Just at the right time, He will come again as God's conquering Warrior to stop the slaughter at Armageddon! "I make known the end from the beginning, from ancient times, what is still to come" (Isa. 46:10).

Whether we understand the timing or not, God's timing is always right. Whether the timing relates to things of the Spirit or elements of everyday life, we must trust that God's timing is always perfect.

Learning to obediently listen to God's guiding voice of timing is imperative. He knows the overall plan and outcome—we don't. "I am God, and there is no other; I am God, and there is none like me" (Isa. 46:9). Sometimes a prophet has to take a very firm stand. I doubt that God would call or choose anyone as a modern-day prophet who has not been seasoned in their walk with the Lord to discern God's timing and also withstand the slings and arrows that may be leveled against them when they speak forth messages from the Lord.

When prophets' personal feelings do not enter or interfere with their mission, their ministry displays maturity. If they will not be dissuaded from their call to speak God's words, God can use them to edify the Body of Christ through the gift of prophecy. In some cases, God will use prophets, pastors, and priests to give a final warning to people that, if gone unheeded, will bring them face to face with their own mortality. In other cases, the word will be gentler and give encouragement where needed. In either case, however, the voice of the Lamb will not be silenced. God will continue to deliver words of warning and of blessing through today's prophets, just as He has done historically.

There is a large black thread woven in the tapestry of Scripture that runs from Genesis to Revelation: it is disobedience. Most books of the Bible reek with accounts of the disobedience of mankind and the consequences thereof. Even so, however, the Scriptures also record that God's redemptive love quenches His anger and vengeance. This love is the golden thread in the tapestry. There is a very prominent red thread woven in stripes across the Old and the New Testaments. This signifies the innocent blood of Christ shed for all mankind. There are many other colors in God's work of art. There is yellow, orange, pink, lavender, and green, which signify the beauty of flowers, trees, and all the grandeur of nature in creation. When God is finished weaving, we will see that the black thread has been pulled out and replaced with a sparkling blue thread, which signifies complete obedience. Then, the tapestry will come to life and become the new heaven, the new earth, and the New Jerusalem, which will come down from above. Never again will there be a black thread of disobedience! Never again will there be jealousy, selfishness, or inflated egos. We will be one in Christ forever.

God's time clock is ticking away! God's heart is beating in time with that clock, and all that is contained in Scripture will be fulfilled in His timing. For now we can trust in His timing for our own lives and for the unfolding of His plan for mankind.

 **A PRAYER**

Dear God, all praise, honor and glory be to You and Your beloved Son. I wait in anticipation for the midnight hour, when the timing of this world and this life is completed according to all Your plans. Then we shall move on into that glorious dawning of a new heaven, a new earth, and a new life that will never end. Then, timing will never be an issue again. Eternity has no measurements involved. Thank You, God, for everything! In Jesus Christ's name, I pray. Amen.

—— ❧ **24** ❧ ——

A 21ST CENTURY PARABLE

The disciples came to him and asked, "Why do you speak to the people in parables?" He replied, "The knowledge of the secrets of the kingdom of heaven has been given to you, but not to them."

—MATTHEW 13:10–11

JESUS OFTEN SPOKE to the people in parables. A parable is a story that illustrates a hidden truth. His stories dealt mostly with farmers, shepherds, and landowners—their finances, religious beliefs, cultural mores, and the like. Jesus' stories contained characters, situations, and settings that were common to the people of His day.

At this juncture I will share a story of my own that uses a subject that is familiar to me. Music has always played a vital part in my life. It was, at one time, almost an obsession for me. I began violin lessons at age 5, and I could read music before I could comprehend "readin' and ritin'." I thought that the pursuit of music would be my life's goal, but God had other ideas regarding His calling for me. I know that someday Jesus will restore my numb, crippled arthritic hands to normal, and that He has a Stradivarius violin (which I never could have afforded in this life) waiting for me. I'm going to play it so much that even the most patient of angels are going to say, "Knock if off—enough is enough!"

THE PARABLE OF THE STRING QUARTET, AND HOW IT GREW

Once there was a very unique Violin, who was so proud of himself, and who was so arrogant about both his construction and tone that he would never agree to anything but being "first" Violin in any performance. He always had to be in the spotlight and on center stage. He always thought that he had to be the one setting the tempo and carrying the melody. Lovely as the "first" Violin's tone sounded, God thought that he had a thin, rather lonely quality, like a wandering spirit who did not quite know where it belonged.

So, the "Great Composer/Conductor" decided to call for a "second" Violin. Suddenly, the depth of beauty contained in the melody became enhanced and enlarged by the counterpart of a sub-melody provided by the exquisite tone of the "second" Violin. God was so pleased with this duet. Then, creative as He is, He decided to call for a Viola, which is slightly larger than a Violin and is tuned one-fifth lower in pitch. It added a soft, velvety, alto/tenor quality to the melody, which was quite appealing to the ear. Wanting to enhance this heavenly music even further, He called for a Cello. This is a violin raging in size and tone between a Viola and a bass Viol. The rich, mellow baritone voice of the Cello made even the angels gather and hang over the celestial fence to listen. The "first" Violin became a bit emotionally "out-of-tune." He felt he had lost his importance and become swallowed up and stirred into a musical stew. Yet, he liked the resulting blend of the quartet enough that he kept playing, with no more audible complaints.

As always, God's mind and creative genius is never stilled. He began to wonder, "What if I added some "reed" instruments to this perfect quartet?" So, He called for some Clarinets. They are single-reed woodwinds that add a clear, bell-like tone and quality to the mix. God was so pleased that He called for some Oboes, who are double-reed woodwinds. They provide a high, penetrating tone of melancholy wherever the "Great Composer/Conductor" chose to write in a touch of longing or sadness to the score. Then He remembered the Saxophones, a one-reed keyed wind instrument with a mellow tone that is so pleasing to hear. "The reeds I have chosen so far sound great," said God. "Now, let's try a Bassoon." This is a double-reed woodwind with a deep, almost gravely bass tone. The other instruments, affectionately, refer to the Bassoon as their musical bedpost. Even though his tone is quite different from the other reeds, God has His own purpose for everything He creates.

God's ingenuity began running at an increased speed, and He called for some Flutes. These are high-pitched wind instruments, whose breathy quality adds to the mystical side of the original melody. Then God said to the Flutes, "Send me your little sons that you call Piccolos." These are small flutes, pitched an octave higher than their papas. Piccolos add a tinkling, impish sound to any performance and come across almost as laughter. Suddenly, God's enthusiasm began to snowball so fast that the ears of the Cherubim and Seraphim barely could keep up with the swelling grandeur of sound. God added the exuberance of the Brass section, which supplied the power base for joy. Maybe that's why Scripture tells of the appearing of Christ at the Rapture as being with a "Trumpet" call of God!

"Oh my goodness," said God, "What is a musical assembly without the percussion group—the Piano, Xylophone, Cymbals, and Drums of all kinds?" The Drums especially can simulate the sound of thunder when called upon to do so. "Oops," said God, "I almost forgot the Harp—the most heavenly of all my strings." No other instrument can play the difficult arpeggios as can the Harp. WOW! Look what the lovely, but lowly string quartet has become by obediently following the musical genius of their Creator. With each addition of instruments, the crescendo of song began building, swelling, and rising until the magnificent sound of a Symphony orchestra crashed through the gate of heaven and bowed before the throne of God with a thrilling cascade of praise, adoration, and thanksgiving!

My story continues with the old saying, "Wherever God builds a church, Satan builds a temple right next door." Ever since the Garden of Eden, Lucifer could be seen hanging around with a glare of jealousy and resentment in his eyes. There was a time when he was the most beautiful and loved angel in heaven. But, then he became the leader of an angelic revolt. He arrogantly thought that he could be God and have everyone worship him. A fierce battle ensued, and he was cast out of heaven and exiled on earth. From that point on, he has been out to get revenge against God. Guess what—his favorite weapon to use against God is mankind, the creation He loves the most. Since this story is presented as a parable, I will continue to use musical instruments in allegorical form.

Satan, being the clever fox that he is, decided to play on the hidden resentment he knew still existed in the "first" Violin, and he convinced him to start playing the measures of music written strictly for the Clarinets. This offended the Clarinets, and made them angry. Suddenly, the Bassoon decided that God didn't give him as many measures to play, and so he began trying to play the parts of the Violins, which turned out to be disastrous. The Grand Piano's ego got the best of him, and he began trying so hard to play the arpeggios, that the Harp performs so easily, that be broke one of his legs and went crashing down to the floor. You can imagine the mess the elephant-sized percussion instrument made on the concert stage. Ivory keys and wire strings were flying everywhere! The Oboe decided that the Flutes and Piccolos were silly little intruders in such a royal orchestra, and he played their measures to show them how he thought it should be done. But the most ridiculous participants in this charade were the dumb and dumber Drums! They thought they could play the Brass Section's music better than the Horns did. To their dismay, the Brass score didn't look remotely like the measures written for Drums and so they stomped back to their corner of the stage and pouted for days.

This rebellion went on and on, like the domino effect that disobedience always causes. What was once the music of heaven suddenly became a cacophony of noise that sounded like an out-of-tune, out-of-tempo, rag-tag street band that was entertaining at the gates of hell. When this happened, God was so disappointed and upset that He closed the doors, windows, and the gate of heaven, and retreated to His throne room. There, He put on His 24-carat gold earmuffs and blocked out the sound of His disobedient creations!

Do you see this story's parallel to what happens when we decide that we know more than God and become hell-bent on doing things our own way? Are we God's celestial Symphony, obediently doing what He created and assigned each one of us to do? Are we using the specific gift He gave each one of us to its fullest potential? Are we adding the beauty of our own gift to the beauty of the gifts of others instead of coveting others' gifts because we think God short-changed us?

If we do not obey God's intentions and expectations for us, then no matter how much we think we are doing God's will—when we are actually doing our own will—our efforts are worth nothing in His eyes. When we don't follow the music of His Word, then He doesn't listen to our music or our prayers either (read Isaiah 1:15). Anyone who tries to rewrite God's notes by changing, adding to, or deleting all or some of them will find that they have created nothing but a Sonata for Satan!

—— **A Prayer** ——

Dear God, all praise and honor be to You and Your Son. Please give us hearts that are open and receptive to Your will being obediently accomplished here on earth. Give us ears to hear the music of heaven, and give us voices to sing your songs and spread Your Holy Word among every nation on earth! We can do nothing right, except by Your guidance. In Jesus' Christ's name, I pray. Amen.

25

THE BIG *IF!*

If my people, who are called by my name, will humble themselves and pray and seek my face and turn from their wicked ways, then will I hear from heaven and will forgive their sin and will heal their land!

—2 Chronicles 7:14

"WHEN SOLOMON HAD finished building the temple of the Lord and the royal palace, and had achieved all he had desired to do, the Lord appeared to him a second time, as he had appeared to him at Gibeon. The Lord said to him: 'I have heard your prayer and plea you have made before me; I have consecrated this temple, which you have built, by putting my Name there forever. My eyes and my heart will always be there'" (1 Kings 9:1–3). Then followed the above promise from God for those who belong to Him.

Second Chronicles 7:14 was referring to Israel and the Jewish people. However, I believe the covenant and promise to

Solomon could also apply to America. The big IF for America receiving this from God is IF we repent and return to the faith, the hope, and the allegiance to God of our founding fathers: if we could just recapture the vision they had for America.

God blessed Abraham and his descendants, and He has most certainly blessed America and her people. We, in America, have basked luxuriously in the abundance Jesus said He came to bring. We have taken his goodness and blessings for granted, however. Nothing we think that what we have worked for and earned is truly ours. We only have our possessions because God is so generous and has given us the chance to make proper use of his bounty. Throughout all Hebrew history, the Jewish people have strayed, becoming lost in other pagan religions and traditions and having earned the anger and rebuke of God. Take a good look, America! We are guilty of the same disobedience! Yet, God's patience and love has always called Israel back, and forgave them again and again. I know, with all my heart, that God will give America the same chance if we will just pull ourselves up out of the pigpen of the prodigal son and come humbly back to Him!

America is slowly being stolen from her constituents, and is being covertly controlled by Satan's henchman, under the clever umbrella called, "The great politically correct society!" Constituent, according to Webster's Dictionary means, "necessary in the formation of the whole; a necessary part of an element." We are rapidly becoming a "pawn" in the political chess game that is destroying the concept of "a government of the people, by the people, and for the people." We are free because of the blood-sacrifice of our sons and daughters from the American War of Independence to the current war in Iraq. Our most fierce enemy is not from beyond our borders; it is from the rot within our nation that was caused by us allowing God's Word to be eradicated from our national life. We are dishonoring those who have died for our diminishing freedoms, and we sit like Rodin's statue *The Thinker*, thinking and thinking, but doing NOTHING! The ACLU and other alphabetical alligators are eating us alive! They have somehow hoodwinked their way into forbidding prayer in schools and banning the display of the Ten Commandments in public places and courtrooms, where of all places, they should be displayed. Now, the latest insult is to try to take the words, "under God" out of our pledge of allegiance!

If we think that "we the people" have much, if any, clout anymore, we are no better off than the "lotus-eaters" of Greek legend. The fruit of the lotus plant puts people in a state of lazy forgetfulness. Most of the decisions of any importance are placed in the hands of the Supreme Court. It seems that everything that God says is a SIN is gaining approval in their court. Because their "absolute authority" is virtually irrevocable, their decisions override the will of the people who cannot even vote on the issues that impact their lives in such critical ways. Once they are appointed, only retirement or death can remove them.

America's Christians, don't you hear God calling you into action? What do you think faith, forgiveness, repentance, and salvation is all about? It doesn't mean we can get away with doing nothing to advance the kingdom of God; that Jesus will do it all. His answer to that fallacy is this, "Partner with Me and make a difference!"

Christians all over the world are longing for the appearance of Christ in the Rapture. Maybe Christ is tarrying so long because there aren't enough true, Spirit-filled Christians to warrant His making that glorious trip. Maybe He's not impressed with the wedding gown (facade) that His bride is intending to wear. Maybe He's disappointed that TOO MANY would have to be left behind if He were to come today.

Never is a word that never should be used to limit God. "With God, all things are possible!"

Ostriches are the largest, non-flying birds in Africa and the Near East. They can run at a remarkable rate of speed. They have a habit of burying their heads in the sand when threatened. Maybe they think that in doing so, the problem will just disappear. If a real enemy were there, they would be chopped off at their long, skinny legs before they knew what happened! I don't think ostriches have too much stored in their attics! What do you think, Christians?

Tombstones often tell a story about the "dearly departed." Here's one epitaph I hope never fits someone you might know.

> Here lie the bones of Tommy Jones,
> Who never did a thing!
> He didn't work—he didn't vote—he never tried to
>   sing!
> He loved himself, but never others—
> Not mother, father, friends, or brothers!
> When people cast God's Word away,
> He didn't have a thing to say.
> One day his lazy heart did stop,
> And down to hell he went – kerplop!

Hypocrites! Christ's favorite description of those who cared only for their own salvation; who were so steeped in their own religiosity that they refused the love Christ extended to them. He stood on the hills above Jerusalem with tears streaming down His cheeks, longing to redeem even those who ridiculed Him. I wonder how often His tears come now, as He sees how little people care about Him and about rescuing His lost lambs.

Israel, the "apple of His eye," the love of His heart for His chosen people, and the longing to gather them again to His bosom. Israel, the land from which came the lineage of His beloved Son, beginning with Abraham. We who have been washed in the blood of the Lamb and are filled with the Spirit of Christ have become a part of that magnificent lineage of the Son of God. God is the Father to both Jews and Christian Gentiles—we cannot be separated!

"Never let love and faithfulness leave you. Bind them together around your neck and write them on the tablet of your heart. Then you will win favor and a good name in the sight of God and men. Trust in the Lord with all your heart and lean not on your own understanding. In all your ways, acknowledge Him, and He will make your path straight" (Prov. 3:3–6, author's paraphrase).

Genesis to Revelation—there is but one theme. "I am God and there is no other" (Isa. 46:8). God is my Father! God's Word, the incarnate Jesus Christ, is my Brother. God, the Holy Spirit, is the unending song of love in my heart.

We must turn our doing "nothing" attitude into doing "something" needed for America to turn her eyes and her heart back to God! God's patience is beyond human understanding, but even God's patience will one day end, maybe sooner than we think.

—— A PRAYER ——

Dear God, all praise, honor, and glory belong to You and our beloved Savior. Please forgive the heresy of some

Americans against Your Holy Word. This great nation was founded on the precepts of Your justice and wisdom, and the faith of our founding fathers. They put their trust in You, and America flourished! In the name of Jesus Christ, please God, shake our people into consciousness and action. Please do not allow us to leave an inheritance, for our children and grandchildren, of bondage in a godless, totalitarian government. Amen.

26

JESUS IS LOVE,
BUT DON'T TAKE HIM
FOR GRANTED

And anyone who does not take his cross and follow me is NOT worthy of me. Whoever finds his life will lose it, and whoever loses his life for my sake will find it. He who receives you receives me, and he who receives me receives the one who sent me. Anyone who receives a prophet because he is a prophet will receive a prophet's reward.
—MATTHEW 10:38–41, EMPHASIS ADDED

All things have been committed to me by my Father. No one knows the Son except the Father, and no one knows the Father except the Son and those to whom the Son chooses to reveal him.
—MATTHEW 11: 27

T HE LOVE OF God for mankind was manifest in the greatest of all gifts that could be given—the birth of His only Son. A beautiful baby boy was delivered of a virgin to bring joy, hope, and redemption to a world gone mad with selfish, cruel, decadent behavior. It was a world filled with greed, hate, war, jealousy, and heartless tyranny. It was a place where human life was expendable, to be used in blood-sport arenas of that day. (The 21st Century must look like déjà vu to God!) This innocent little boy named Jesus was literally "born to die."

God is a love story so deep, so broad, and so mysterious that He goes beyond the comprehension of mankind. In spite of the fact that today's world is crumbling from disgusting behavior that are products of casting away of God's Word and is trembling from the fear of terrorism, there is a beautiful and delicate balance of "good" present on the face of this planet. The Spirit of Christ is alive, just as Christ, Himself, is alive. He is, and always has been, the good that exists. He promised He would never leave us, and by His Spirit, He never has.

It's time for serious reflection on what Christ's appearance on earth really meant, and what it means today. Troublesome as the world has become since the birth of Christ over two thousand years ago, He has fulfilled His promises. He clearly stated that His followers would do even greater things than He did. Jesus knew that great medical breakthroughs would come, that the computer age would come via satellites suspended in space, and that the harnessing of electricity and assembly lines would usher in the manufacturing age. He knew that cars, planes, and spaceships would transport people to new frontiers at ever rapid rates, that scientific knowledge in many diverse areas would blossom, and that technology would just keep growing and expanding. These miraculous powers, when used for the good of mankind, are some of the ways in which Jesus' prophecy was fulfilled.

God did not give us these abilities to exalt any man. Instead, He gave us the inventive genius of His own mind to benefit the whole world. He gave us the music of heaven through the sensitivity of Bach, Beethoven, Mozart, and countless others. The Renaissance awakened the art world to produce paintings that would be cherished for all time. Charity and caring for the less fortunate would never have come into being, except for the heart of Christ. We are the vessels through which God works His miracles in every nation on earth.

Not all of the creative geniuses on this planet believe in God. In spite of this, God still even uses the talents of unbelievers to fulfill His purposes for mankind. All abilities, even those of the atheists, are from God. He is the Giver of all talents and ingenuity, and He uses them for the good of others. God uses believers and unbelievers alike. Nothing created by God goes to waste.

God's Word is not given to condemn us, but rather, it is meant to "awaken the sleeper" and bid them to open the door of their hearts to allow the Spirit of Christ to come in.

People are so starved for spiritual encounters with God that they think they see images of Christ or the Virgin Mary in strange places like tree stumps, gnarls in the wood of a door, or in the dirt smeared on a window that should have been washed weeks ago. It is up to us to point them toward having an encounter with the one and only Savior, Jesus Christ. What they need is for Christ's Holy Spirit to live in their hearts. The depth of His love in the human heart brings such joy, peace, and true knowledge of the living Christ that chasing after images becomes a thing of the past. Christians who are still chasing after these images need to consider the possibility that these apparitions are from Satan, the father of lies who takes great pleasure in confusing believers. Jesus warned that in the latter days the very elect would be fooled. If believers in Christ can be attracted to such nonsense now, what is going to happen to them when the "beast" described in the Book of Revelation appears on the scene?

Not everyone who sits every Sunday in a church pew is going to be taken up in the Rapture. A great deception is unfolding even today. The Antichrist will be a man of dynamic intellect. He will have the power to solve many problems. He will have such a charismatic personality that he will charm the whole world. He will perform miracles, and he will bring a few years of false peace and prosperity which the weary world so desperately longs to have. By the time people wake up and realize that this charlatan is Satan himself, it will be too late and many will prefer death to living under the barbaric demands of his regime. If our faith is now only based on what we can see or feel, or on the good deeds we lay claim to, then we are being set up to be fooled by the Antichrist.

God is calling all of us to the safety of spiritual maturity. His voice calling is not imaginary. Listen! It is the voice of God calling to bring His children safely home. Playtime is over—it's suppertime—the feast already is prepared, and the royal goblets are filled to the brim When Christ has turned water into wine, He always saves the best wine for last.

A PRAYER

Dear God, all praise and thanksgiving be to You and Your Son. Let us cast away all the mistakes of the past and humbly come to You, willing to let You enter our hearts with Your Spirit and change us into new people, guided only by You. Awaken us to the knowledge that new wine cannot be poured into old wineskins! We ask all things in Jesus' name. Amen.

—— ❦ 27 ❦ ——

NOT ALL IDOLS ARE
SILVER AND GOLD

Praise the Lord, for the Lord is good; sing praise to his
name, for that is pleasant. I know that the Lord is great,
that our Lord is greater than all gods. The Lord does
whatever pleases him, in the heavens and the earth, in
seas and all their depths. He makes clouds rise from the
ends of the earth; he sends lightening with the rain and
brings out the wind from his storehouses. Your name,
O Lord, endures forever, your renown, O Lord, through
all generations. For the Lord will vindicate His people
and have compassion on His servants. The idols of the
nations are silver and gold, made by the hands of men.
They have mouths, but cannot speak, eyes, but they
cannot see; they have ears, but cannot hear, nor is there
breath in their mouths. Those who make them will be
like them, and so will all who trust in them.
—PSALM 135:3, 5–7, 13–18

AT TIMES GOD'S people have misused and twisted His
genius for their own glory and destructive purposes.

Most of earth's problems, whether on an international
level or on an individual level, can be traced to some latent,
devilish desire to have more than what God has already
given to us. We long to have that material possession or
special talent that has been afforded someone else. For some
reason, the grass always looks greener on the other side of
the fence, even though the grass needs to be mowed no

matter what side of the fence we are on.

God, in harmony with Christ's prophecy that man would do greater things than He did, has blessed this planet with abundant knowledge. God's creative mind has enlightened us to the point that many believe we don't need God's guidance anymore. They have conveniently forgotten that all that mankind has accomplished initially came from our Creator. In the western world, even those who recognize from where our blessings flow must be careful not to become so used to our comforts that we lose our awe of Him because we are in awe of the abundance around us. When this happens, our praise of Him becomes ritualistic rather than heartfelt. We must be careful that our relationship with Him does not render us deserving of the assessment: "These people honor me with their lips, but their hearts are far from me" (Matt. 15:8).

Mankind has become so "smart" that we have slipped off God's golden path and produced hurtful things alongside beneficial things. We have learned to turn the manufacturing of plows and pitchforks into guns and bullets. Along with the discovery of curative medicines, we have developed deadly bacterial bombs and killer gasses that could wipe out one-third of earth's population in the momentary madness of one individual.

Idols of today are still rooted in the love of money, but they are far more complex and confusing than the selling and worship of statues made of silver and gold. The golden calves of today often are in the making and worship of the money made by misusing the creativity God has allotted to man.

Idols also take the form of land. Nations are in constant conflict because they want more than what their own borders entitle them to have. Palestinians intend to take over Israel, make Jerusalem their capitol, and if possible, drive the Jewish people out. This will not happen because God gave this tiny nation, Israel, to the Jews. He has called them home from every corner of the earth. Israel is theirs and anyone who attempts to conquer or destroy the land of the Jews will be cursed and will meet with God's divine supernatural destruction. Arafat is dead, and he betrayed the Jewish people and the world with false promises of peace. Israel and the world must be vigilant in prayer that someone with similar or worse intentions will not succeed him. While it is true that we must keep striving for peace, it is also true that we cannot afford to wear rose-colored glasses that will distort our view of reality.

As it is written, so shall it be. It is truly ludicrous that so many people from so many nations think they can stop God's will from being fulfilled. God has clearly stated in Scripture that Christ will be seated on David's throne at Jerusalem, and He will reign as King of Kings and Lord of Lords for one thousand years. Intelligent people are absolutely ignorant when they do not read and adhere to God's Word.

It is time to wake up. The internal composition of this weary old earth is groaning and moaning. Fault lines beneath the substrata are shifting and moving. The seas are churning and exploding onto land. The mountains are growling and stoking up their bottomless furnaces. Rains and melting snow are causing rivers and lakes to flood their banks and destroy everything in their path. The *Titanic* sank by crashing into an iceberg. Now, it's a gigantic iceberg that has broken loose and will be the one that crashes—only God knows where and what the consequences may be. It's as if the entire planet is rebelling against the unrepentant disobedience of mankind toward our Creator. All these disasters we are seeing now, with increasing intensity, are just the outer edge of tribulation. The "Great Tribulation," which will come after the church has been raptured, will be beyond description. If people describe our earth as a "dog-eat-dog" world now, wait until the indwelling of Christ's Holy Spirit has "left the building!" Jesus said, "And when these things begin to come to pass, then look up, and lift up your heads; for your redemption draweth nigh" (Luke 21:28, KJV).

The blood sports in the arenas of biblical days have now become the blood-sport arenas of our city streets and schools. We have allowed God, His Word, and His commandments to be eradicated from our schools and public life. God have mercy on our children, because too many have not been given any kind of moral or spiritual guidance. Many times our families are too busy trying to pile up silver and gold so that they can buy their children the luxury items they want to show them how much they are loved. The real love they need is in teaching them, by example, to be responsible for their actions, to be resourceful in solving life's problems, and to be conscious of the needs of others—all for the sake of Christ. When silver and gold becomes our idol—or obsession, we lose more than our eyes to see, our ears to hear, and our breath to speak: we lose our beloved children.

Wake up: Praise the Lord! Take your faith seriously. Lead as many to Christ as you possibly can, *today*. Time is winding down, and tomorrow may be too late. Don't be like Scarlet O'Hara who always had the philosophy of, "After all, tomorrow is another day." It's quite possible that tomorrow will never come, because you were not doing God's will today. Eternal life is not a prize to be won at the spin of some spiritual wheel of fortune—it is a gift that has been given to us at a price which not one person on the face of this earth would be willing, or qualified, to pay.

——— A PRAYER ———

Dear God, all praise and honor be to You and our beloved Savior. Fill our hearts with such passion and power of the Holy Spirit that we cannot be lured away from your kingdom by the dazzle of silver and gold idols of this world. Let your will be done on earth as it is in heaven! In Jesus' name we pray. Amen.

—— ≪ 28 ≫ ——

MY HELP COMES FROM
THE LORD

I will lift up mine eyes unto the hills, from whence cometh my help. My help cometh from the Lord, which made heaven and earth. He will not suffer thy foot to be moved: he that keepeth thee will not slumber. Behold, he that keepeth Israel shall neither slumber nor sleep. The Lord is thy keeper: the Lord is thy shade upon thy right hand. The sun shall not smite thee by day, nor the moon by night. The Lord shall preserve thee from all evil: he shall preserve thy soul. The Lord shall preserve thy going out and thy coming in from this time forth, and even for evermore.

—PSALM 121, KJV

THIS PSALM IS one of the guiding forces of my life! Whenever I need time out to relax and refresh my spirit, these words automatically come into my consciousness. After I end my prayers with, "In Jesus' name, Amen," I always follow with Psalm 121. This bolsters my strength, my peace, and my purpose for the rest of the day, because I really believe that what God says He will do, and He does!

This being the final chapter of this book, I wish to express my hopes that those who read it may be awakened to the knowledge of how much God loves them! I hope it opens some windows to the fact that there is so much more to

Christian faith than many understand. I hope it instills in the reader's heart a longing to transcend from level to level, from glory to glory, in spiritual cognizance, until it literally bursts forth as the heart of a newborn son or daughter in Christ! I hope this book lights a candle that can never be extinguished in someone's heart! I hope the Word of God becomes the very core of existence for many! I hope that I have, at least partially, fulfilled my calling from God to faithfully deliver his messages as He gives them to me. "For I have lifted His cross; His glorious banner unfurled and went forth with Christ by my side!"

The true church of Christ is entering a dynamic new era of PASSION! Many may not sense it yet, but I am feeling it with every spiritual nerve in my soul. Soon, the "many" will also wake up to this miraculous reality. However, be aware, just as believers will work harder to establish God's kingdom, so will Satan and his henchmen work harder to interfere. We are already seeing his clawed hand in the world! Satan's hand is in the wars; starvation; AIDS; murder of Christians in various countries; all kinds of dangerous problems from animals, birds, and insects that could affect humans with grave illnesses; terrorists; disastrous upheavals of nature; and the turning against God by many nations—to name just a few.

The most devious, subtle attacks that Satan will make, however, are going to occur in the church against the true church (body of Christ)! He will place false prophets and teachers everywhere he thinks he can get away with the spewing out of "sweet sounding myths" that will destroy belief in the true teachings of God's holy Word and encourage regard for Jesus Christ as just a historical figure, and a pathetic one at that. This is not something that is suddenly happening. Satan has been working his hateful mischief for many years, in many diverse places, through many naïve people! The church has gone merrily on its way, playing spiritual "blind-man's-bluff," and now when the blindfold has been taken off, they are shocked by what they see happening all around them!

God is a good God and as long as we still have one breath of life left in us, we still have a chance to repent, give our lives to Him, and fulfill His will here on earth. We have time to "kiss the Son" and love Him. All praise, honor, and glory must be given to the Father, Son, and Holy Spirit now and into infinity!

—— A PRAYER ——

Dear God, now that the end of this particular book has come, my prayer is that it will be just the beginning of a new vision for those who may read it. My hope is that they will comprehend the fullness of its message, as well as the depth of meaning in all of your holy Scripture. The journey on the road to heaven may not always be easy, but nevertheless, it is a joyous journey because of the knowledge that Christ is waiting for us, just around the last bend in the road. In Jesus' name, I pray. Amen.